POINT OF PURCHASE
D·E·S·I·G·N 2

POINT OF PURCHASE
D·E·S·I·G·N 2

Robert B. Konikow

PBC International, Inc., New York

Distributor to the book trade in the United States and Canada:

Rizzoli International Publications, Inc.
597 Fifth Avenue
New York, NY 10017

Distributor to the art trade in the United States:

Letraset USA
40 Eisenhower Drive
Paramus, NJ 07653

Distributor to the art trade in Canada:

Letraset Canada Limited
555 Alden Road
Markham, Ontario L3R 3L5, Canada

Distributed throughout the rest of the world by:

Hearst Books International
105 Madison Avenue
New York, NY 10016

Library of Congress Cataloging-in-Publication Data

Konikow, Robert B.

   Point of purchase design 2.

   Includes indexes.
      1. Advertising, Point-of-sale.   2. Display of
merchandise.   I. Title   II. Title: Point of purchase
design two.

HF5845.K719 1989   659.1'57   88-31389
ISBN 0-86636-074-3

Color separations, printing and binding by
Toppan Printing Co. (H.K.) Ltd.

Typesetting by
Jeanne Weinberg Typesetting

PRINTED IN HONG KONG
10 9 8 7 6 5 4 3 2 1

STAFF

Managing Director	Penny Sibal-Samonte
Financial Director	Pamela McCormick
Creative Director	Richard Liu
Associate Art Director	Daniel Kouw
Editorial Manager	Kevin Clark
Artist	Kim McCormick

CONTENTS

FOREWORD

Here it is. You hold in your hands the second collection of point-of-purchase displays that I have been privileged to have worked on. I hope you are as pleased by this book as you were by the first, and find it as interesting and valuable. I have found putting it together a rewarding experience.

Valuable? In what way is such a book valuable? How are you likely to use it? What will your reaction to it be? These are questions that are of great interest to an author. The answers tell him whether he has done a good job, and whether his efforts have resulted in something that is considered worthwhile.

Our experience with the first book in this series, and with other volumes we have produced for the Library of Applied Design, indicates that there are a number of ways in which these collections have served their buyers, and some of these might be of interest to the new reader.

The most obvious is esthetic pleasure, the ease of seeing in one place nearly 400 examples of top-quality displays. To anyone who is involved in any aspect of the point-of-purchase industry, the book tends to act as an affirmation of the importance of the endeavor in which we are all engaged. There is a special reward for those advertisers, producers, and designers, whose work has been included in the book. Appearance here is a symbol of recognition, of acceptance, and I know, from what people have told me, that there is a sense of pride at having one's work included here.

But the book has proved itself to be more widely useful than as a boost to the egos of those whose work is included. All creative people are constantly looking for ideas. Writers are rarely without a notebook, or at least a piece of blank paper, on which they are constantly jotting down notes of ideas that come to them, of snatches of conversation that they overhear in restaurants or elevators, of signs they see or incidents they notice—all grist for the mill, and the stuff of which future writing may be made. Artists are ready to sketch an interesting face they see in the subway, an unusual facade. Architects will notice details of buildings, unusual ways of solving a problem, and keep them for future reference.

Designers will build up collections of work they like and keep them for reference as idea starters. In the vernacular, they are called "swipe files," and they are a valuable asset which grow with the years. For many designers, books like this act as a swipe file. When embarking on a new project, a new assignment, one of the early steps in developing a solution is to leaf through collections of ideas—tearsheets from your own files, or the pages of this book—until something sparks the imagination, starts the creative juices flowing, and a solution gets under way.

Another use to which these books have been put, and this was somewhat of a revelation to me, was as a communications bridge. Many people on the client side turn out to be more or less visually illiterate. They may know what they want in the way of design, but they have difficulty expressing this in words, and they are certainly not capable of sketching out their feelings. In talking to an account executive, the client outlines his wishes in words, the rep returns to the designer and interprets what he thinks the client wants. The designer does a sketch which goes back to the client, and far too often, it is wide of the mark. Words have not been an effective means of communication.

A more effective way, it seems, is to use this book to help the client tell what direction he wants to pursue. When he indicates his preference, the rep can leaf through the pages until he finds something that he thinks comes close to the client's description, and gets the client's response. Or the client can search through the illustrations until he sees something that falls in the correct category, something that has the feeling he is looking for. There is no need for slavish imitation, but the client's selection will serve as a better guide for the designer, and cut down on the time needed to reach a satisfactory solution.

If there are any other ways in which this book has been useful to you, or if there are things we can do to make it better and more useful, both the publisher and I would be interested in hearing from you.

Robert B. Konikow

INTRODUCTION

What is point-of-purchase advertising?

It is difficult to generalize about this dynamic medium. If you were to leaf through this book without prior experience with the medium, you would probably find it difficult to decide what these hundreds of objects have in common, and what it is they share that make them eligible for inclusion.

It isn't size, since they vary from objects small enough to be hidden by the hand to those that fill a wall. It isn't material, since almost every conceivable substance may be used, from sheets of paper to wood or metal or plastic. It certainly isn't the nature of the advertiser, for the medium is used for almost every category of product.

The key lies in its name. What all of the units pictured here have in common is that they are designed to be used at the point where the purchase can be made, where interest in the product can be turned immediately into action, where desire can be changed into fulfillment, and where the end result is satisfaction.

Because point-of-purchase advertising is so flexible and so varied, its producers are free to experiment. A newspaper or magazine ad must be designed to fit the limitations of the printing press; a television ad ends up on film or tape; but point-of-purchase advertising, since it is self-contained, is limited only by the ingenuity of its designer and by the economics of the market. Of all the media, it is the first to be able to adopt new technological advances.

For that reason, it is considered a new, modern, medium. But in fact, it is one of the oldest media of commercial communication. As soon as society began to develop, as soon as specialists began to arrive on the scene, there developed a need for a way to let people know where they could obtain specific products. The division of labor forced the man who made shoes for a living to indicate that his house or shop was where others could come to trade their goods or services for his shoes. Perhaps the shoemaker first stationed somebody outside his door to call out his wares, but soon a sign, painted or carved, on the front of the house, told the same story at less cost. Since most people were illiterate, these signs used pictures to tell their message. A gloved hand for a glover, a bunch of grapes for a vintner, were typical. Signs like these were uncovered in the ruins of ancient Pompeii.

The next step was to paint these pictures on slabs of wood, and hang them at right angles to the wall, so they could be seen from a distance. Taverns in England used this kind of sign, often with very elaborate symbolism, and they are still in use. Other signs were three-dimensional. A carved boot or a fully shaped head of a hog made clear the nature of the business within. The Medici's coat of arms contained three golden balls, and this symbol, translated into three dimensions, still indicates a pawn-broker, the inheritor of the Medici tradition. The red-and-white pole which we recognize as the sign of the barber derives from the early function of this tradesman, then a barber/surgeon whose main thera-peutic technique was bloodletting.

In its physical aspects, point-of-purchase advertising is more varied than any other advertising medium.

Television, today's dominant medium if you measure dominance by money invested or by the number of impressions, offers an exciting combination of pictures that move, bright colors, music, voice, and sound effects, as well as a choice of photographic and animation techniques. It is a tremendously creative medium, with almost infinite possibilities, but it all ends up as a reel of motion picture film or videotape which appears on a rectangular screen in the home. And the production cost is high.

Newspaper and magazine ads offer great creative scope, too, but with few exceptions they end up as words and illustrations printed on a piece of flat paper and distributed as part of a publication.

Direct mail adds the possibility of unusual die-cutting and folding, as well as the use of three-dimensional objects, and can thus be more varied and often more exciting. But it must still conform to postal regulations and be suitable for these distribution channels.

Outdoor advertising, via bill-boards, is often used close to the point of purchase, but it is essentially flat, although some attempts at a third dimension have been attempted. Because of mechanical limitatons, it is used in a few standardized sets of dimensions.

Point-of-purchase advertising, however, is almost entirely free of physical limitations. It can cover the whole gamut of physical size from a small decal that goes on a store window to a massive rotating sign in a service station that requires a crane and a crew of construction workers for installation.

A point-of-purchase display can be flat, in bas-relief, or in full-round sculpture. It can be intended for use indoors or outdoors. It can be designed to stand on the floor, on a table or counter, attached to a wall, or hung from a ceiling. It can utilize every technique to reach people through any of their senses —color, light, motion, sound, touch, and even scent—to attract attention and to help convey its message.

The unifying factor that makes point-of-purchase a single entity, that gives it a unity, is simply its location. Any advertising medium that is placed at or near the place where the purchase is made automatically falls into the point-of-purchase category. Its placement is what counts, and the development of how to do this most effectively at this crucial point in the chain that leads to the buying decision is the factor which has brought together the wide variety of skills and crafts that may be seen at any of the annual POPAI exhibits, or the examples of the designers' skills represented in this volume.

COMMUNICATING VALUE THROUGH PROMOTION

JULIE A. MURRAY
Manager, Sales Promotion
Boulevard Distillers and Importers Inc.
NEW YORK, NY

As with all consumer goods marketers, those of us in the wine and spirits industry are emerging from a tumultuous decade for the brandline and selling of products. Certainly we are now facing a new and exciting decade which will require us to review and rethink many of our promotional and display strategies. And while many of the current trends go back several years, many are just emerging.

Some of the most pertinent trends that will have an effect on our planning for the coming years are greater control by the volume retailers, larger stores with fewer salespeople, husbands and wives sharing the shopping responsibilities, more buying decisions being made at the point-of-sale, and an overall desire on the part of the consumer to move through the stores at a greater speed than ever before.

I believe that the successful point-of-sale strategies that deals with these trends will have to tie together regional retailer and consumer needs with the desired national brand image. In addition, promotional displays need to provide a consumer service and help the retailer with additional merchandising opportunities.

In the early eighties, the wine and spirit industry was very much a part of the deregulation era. The most visible effect on what is still a highly regulated industry was the rapid increase in promotions that focused on cents off, in-store and mail-in coupons, rebates and the like. The question at every level— consumer, retailer, distributor, and manufacturer—was how low and, of course, how often is enough. Every time we thought we had seen it all, a new "deal" came along for brands at every level of the price/image scale. While the dust has settled somewhat, there is still a clamor for more price-oriented promotions. Very few brands, one of which is our own Wild Turkey, have been able to stand above the refund battleground.

Beneath this refund/discount hoopla, we are currently seeing a growing counter consumer trend. Quality and value are again gaining strength as we sell less but "better." Consumers are realizing that real discounts are rare and they more often than not select brands that provide value over and above that gained through the use of the product. As brand marketers, we know that there is much to be gained by promoting "value added." The very least to be gained is the benefit of building a brand-loyal franchise rather than stealing dubious consumers from our competition.

Within the promotional display mix, "value added" means working more effectively than ever before. As our retailers and consumers become better informed and educated, they will also become more demanding and selective, having lived through the mass market phenonemon, the deluge of look-alike promotions and point-of-sale material—the discount of the week.

Certainly as we become effective, we will be rewarded. We can expect to see rising demand for quality program material that can last four, five, or six weeks, not just for two or less. This will tie in more closely with consumer purchasing cycles, and mean less work for the retailer.

Working in tandem with being more effective is the need to develop promotions which work both on a regional basis with a national idea as well as over time. These promotions, like our Wild Turkey Discover America campaign, are built around a single theme and support established objectives.

The Wild Turkey Discover America programs have given us greater point-of-purchase versatility by bringing together different interests—American travel, active or passive participation in the American outdoors, and a desire on the part of our consumers to know more about their country. Value is generated by tying our brand with information in either video or pamphlet form on how to plan and where to go to find a wide variety of activities and interests. In addition, a themed premium promotion offer generates greater excitement, and there are many valuable regional and local public relations events that can expand Wild Turkey's Discover America impact.

In total, to meet the '90s effectively our promotions must fully communicate value and must help our retailers merchandise better through ideas, offers, or premium tie-ins that reflect our consumers' needs and desires. We must deemphasize programs that rely on quick discounts or "glitzy" displays that just promote sweepstakes or contests in order to gain attention at the expense of building a loyal consumer and a supportive retailer base.

Advertiser: Air France
Producer: Einson-Freeman Inc., Paramus, NJ

As part of a promotion that gave away 115 round trips for two to Paris, consumers were urged to fill out an entry form at their travel agent, and drop it in the box that was at the base of an Eiffel Tower display. Removing the decorations from the box turned it into a pre-paid mailer to return the entries to Air France.

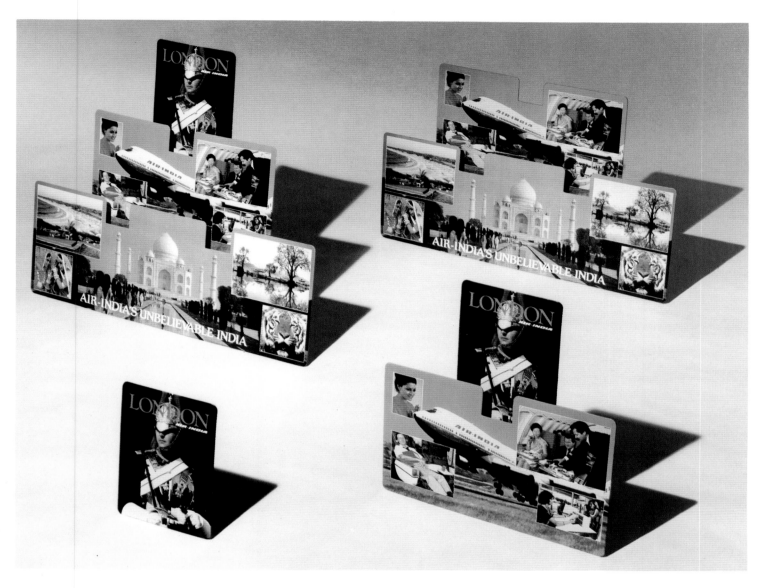

Advertiser: Air India
Producer: Rothchild Printing Co. Inc.,
          Elmhurst, NY

This counter display, showing
destinations reached by Air India,
consists of three pieces, which can
be used individually or in
combination.

Advertiser: Amtrak
Producer: Marketing Displays Inc.,
Farmington Hills, MI

This modular travel display comes with floorstand base, detachable feet, and built-in D-rings, for use on counter, floor, wall, or in a window. Designed to be rotated among travel agencies, they are easily transported due to the light aluminum construction.

Advertiser: American Honda Motorcycle
Producer: Trenmark, La Mirada, CA

The slim design of this unit makes it possible to hang product from the slat wall, and still position the display next to the corresponding bike on the showroom floor.

Advertiser: Dunlop
Producer: David Brace Displays Inc., Lancaster, NY

This merchandising program is unified by a consistent use of graphics, built around the design from the familiar checkerboard flag from the race track, surrounded by a red and a yellow stripe. The program includes an illuminated sign, a clock, stands for tires, and a sales pedestal.

Advertiser: Dunlop
Producer: David Brace Displays Inc.,
Lancaster, NY

This merchandising program is unified by a consistent use of graphics, built around the design from the familiar checkerboard flag from the race track, surrounded by a red and a yellow stripe. The program includes an illuminated sign, a clock, stands for tires, and a sales pedestal.

Advertiser: General Electric Co.
Producer: Creative Displays Inc., Chicago

A not very glamorous product is given an attractive setting in this cabinet that can stand on a counter. The dividers are easily moved to permit each store to distribute space as needed.

Advertiser: Chrysler Corp
Producer: Marketing Displays Inc., Farmington Hills, MI

Designed for dealer parts and service departments, these are made of interlocking panels and tracks, allowing the messages to be presented in any order and combination. The displays can be mounted on the wall or from the ceiling, to fit any dealership layout.

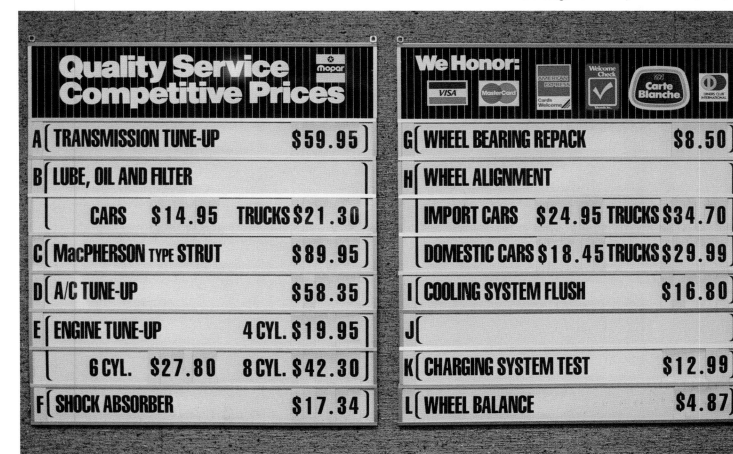

Quality Service Competitive Prices — mopar

A	TRANSMISSION TUNE-UP	$59.95
B	LUBE, OIL AND FILTER	
	CARS $14.95	TRUCKS $21.30
C	MacPHERSON TYPE STRUT	$89.95
D	A/C TUNE-UP	$58.35
E	ENGINE TUNE-UP	4 CYL. $19.95
	6 CYL. $27.80	8 CYL. $42.30
F	SHOCK ABSORBER	$17.34

We Honor: VISA, MasterCard, AMERICAN EXPRESS Cards Welcome, Welcome Check, Carte Blanche, DINERS CLUB INTERNATIONAL

G	WHEEL BEARING REPACK	$8.50
H	WHEEL ALIGNMENT	
	IMPORT CARS $24.95	TRUCKS $34.70
	DOMESTIC CARS $18.45	TRUCKS $29.99
I	COOLING SYSTEM FLUSH	$16.80
J		
K	CHARGING SYSTEM TEST	$12.99
L	WHEEL BALANCE	$4.87

Advertiser: Chrysler International
Producer: Chicago Show, Chicago

This series of related pieces was
designed to enhance the image
and product awareness of both the
Chrysler and Jeep images in both
Europe and the Far East. The
elements were designed to meet
European marketing conditions,
which are somewhat different from
those met in the United States.

Smoked acrylic free-standing units and wall pieces, combined with high-quality photography, convey an upscale, contemporary image. Adhesive feature stickers, window striping, poster signage and warranty stickers complete the package. The etched pentastar on each piece gives immediate identification. In Europe, the kits are made in German, French and English to address unique market segments.

Advertiser: Champion Spark Plug
Producer: Chicago Show, Chicago

This modular program has great flexibility and versatility to accommodate various in-store situations, with a strong, consistent look. It includes promotional poster frames, menu boards, clocks, moving message signs, and gondola signs. Varied assortments were offered dealers, including a promotional package made up of the Champion Racing Girl and a variety of poster inserts.

Advertiser: Ford Motor Co.
Producer: Chicago Show, Chicago

Designed for the dealer floor, this unit offers information on credit plans and current finance specials. A programmable moving message unit offers the dealers flexibility, the graphics can be changeable, and the literature rack can handle brochures of all sizes. In addition, the unit is easily moved to any location on the floor. Related units can be used for coverage on the walls, windows, or the floor.

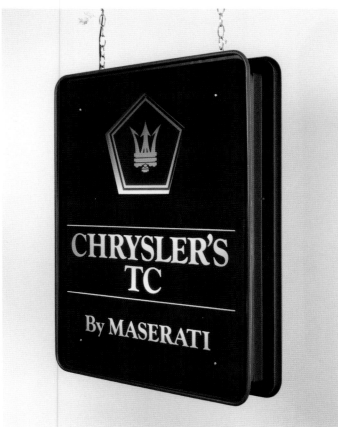

Advertiser: Chrysler Corporation
Producer: Chicago Show, Chicago

The new car produced by Chrysler and Maserati is an upscale car, with only 300 dealerships carrying the new line. So while signage had to reflect the quality and image of the car, the limited run was a challenge. This large, attention-getting, hanging sign was the solution.

Advertiser: Chrysler International
Producer: Chicago Show, Chicago

Dealers needed a compact, efficient way to handle audio-visual equipment for internal training purposes. This unit holds desired combinations of monitor, videodisc player, VCR, and computer, in a secure manner and in a limited space. It can be used for individual training or in a group situation.

Advertiser: Cobra Electronics Group
Producer: The Acorn Group, Chicago
Designer: James Lauro

This counter unit, made of formed styrene, achieves a feeling of permanence. The units are firmly secured to the display, without impeding access for demonstration. Note how product features are listed for each model.

Advertiser: Conoco Inc.
Producer: Marketing Displays Inc.,
Farmington Hills, MI

To establish brand identity with a consistent, contemporary look throughout a chain of jobber-owned stations, a series of related items were developed, including merchandisers, pump-toppers, store-front fascia frames, curb signs, and column cladding, all with universal mountings. Front-loading poster grip frames allow messages to be installed quickly and rotated regularly.

Advertiser: Rugged Trails
Producer: Lawless Display, North Tonawanda, NY
Designer: Bernie Baszak

How do you sell a product that is too big to be shown on the dealership floor? One way is to produce a scale model and use it as the central part of a floor or counter display.

THE CUTTING EDGE?

Of all the industries covered in this book, transportation, and especially, the new car segment, is likely to be the one in which technological developments will appear first. There are a number of reasons for this.

- A new car is a high ticket item. After the purchase of a house, it is probably the largest family purchase.

- It is a complex piece of machinery, with a wide range of options available to the customer. While some, like body color, are obvious, others are hidden and highly technical.

- There is an unusual emotional relationship between a man (and often a woman) and the car that is bought.

- While there may be special promotional offers that run a comparatively short time, the essential product changes very little, if at all, during a model year, so that point-of-purchase displays can have a longer than usual life than is customary for the p-o-p industry.

- The relationship between the manufacturer and its dealers is not only a close one, but often one of long standing. The degree of response to a promotional offer is reasonably predictable.

- There are only a handful of manufacturers, and each is large and substantial. In addition, it is difficult for a new company to enter the market, so there is a fair degree of predictability about who is involved in the competitive picture.

As a result of these factors, the new technologies of display are most likely to make sense and be welcomed in the promotion of automobiles. Not only does the complex story that must be told demand more complicated ways of presenting information, but also these ways are affordable. So we are beginning to see displays that involve the customer, that interact with him to help him find the answers to technical questions, that speed up his understanding of product appearance and engineering features, that seem more convincing and reliable than the word of a salesman.

One example of this recent development was the distribution of a computer disk by Buick. This was a disk, specially prepared for Buick, that outlined the features of all its models for the current year. When I played this promotional disk on my MAC SE, I was able to list and study all the features of all the models being offered. I could compare models, and even get explanations of how some of the more technical features worked. The disk used animation and sound to attract my attention. I heard the motor revving, and even heard how its sound changed when I stepped on the accelerator.

I could select my options and determine how much the car of my dreams would cost. I could print out the itemized costs, and find out how much a month I would have to pay for what I wanted—and then I could start to diddle with options to bring the car within my reach. It was a powerful introduction to the new Buicks, and even though I wasn't in the current market for a new car, it was fascinating.

It was an example of a hi-tech device effectively adapted to promotion. It's the sort of thing that has much wider application than the new car field, but it is only this industry that has the need and the resources to invest in this tool of the future.

Advertiser: Adolph Coors Co.
Producer: Graphic Communications, Golden, CO
Designer: Larry L. Fortner

Using a real dog bowl, this counter display promotes Extra Gold, and can be filled with the dealer's choice of snack foods.

Advertiser: Adolph Coors Co.
Producer: Graphic Communications, Golden, CO
Designer: Larry L. Fortner

This seasonal display, which presents a schedule for the local baseball team, is a creative departure from the standard flat schedule card.

Advertiser: Adolph Coors Co.
Producer: Graphic Communications, Goldon, CO
Designer: Larry L. Fortner

This Beerwolf cut-out stands on a pile of 20 cases of the product, and holds a pricing card to attract impulse sales.

Advertiser: Adolph Coors Co.
Producer: Graphic Communications,
Golden, CO
Designer: Larry L. Fortner

These units, hung from the ceiling,
attract attention through motion.
Some of them are moved by air
currents. The two with the large
circular piece have built-in battery
motors that provide motion.

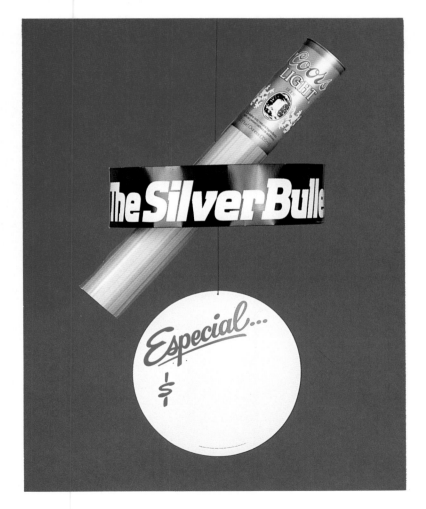

Advertiser: Adolph Coors Co.
Producer: Graphic Communications,
Golden, CO
Designer: Larry L. Fortner

These units, hung from the ceiling, attract attention through motion. Some of them are moved by air currents. The two with the large circular piece have built-in battery motors that provide motion.

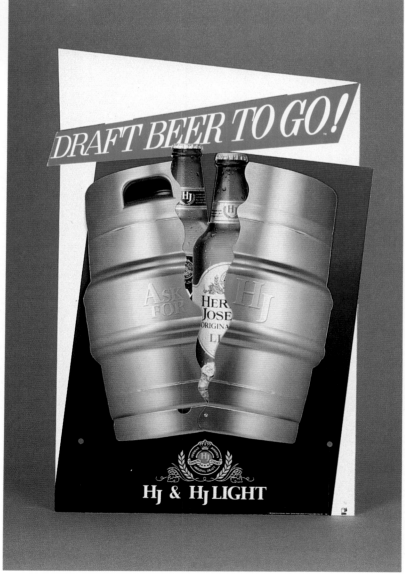

Advertiser: Adolph Coors Co.
Producer: Graphic Communications, Golden, CO
Designer: Larry L. Fortner

This motorized display promotes the fact that the canned Herman Joseph's beers are the same beer that you can get from the keg. The kegs open, showing the two products, regular and light, emerging.

Advertiser: Adolph Coors Co.
Producer: Graphic Communications,
           Golden, CO
Designer: Larry L. Fortner

A series of four displays were developed to dispense Coors Light Beerwolf sports posters. Each display holds 100 posters and comes fully packed with pop-up header, and an easel that folds out from the rear.

Advertiser: Anheuser-Busch Inc.
Producer: Visual Marketing Inc., Chicago
Designer: Dennis Nielsen

Building on the popularity of the Chicago Bears in the Chicago market, a promotion was developed built around a serving tray whose art work used the widely-known "Monsters of the Midway" graphic. Consumers were offered the 1988 tray for $3.95 with a proof of purchase. The tray was also used as a dealer-loader. Wholesalers could buy the trays in case lots, to be distributed as a wall plaque, or even as serving trays. All elements were four-color process.

Advertiser: Heileman's Old Style
Producer: Thomas A. Schutz Co., Inc.,
Morton Grove, IL
Designer: Ronald P. Eckert

Designed to be used for Lone Star and Rainier beers, as well as Old Style, this pool table lamp simulated stained glass through the use of printed vacuum forming. The shaped art work was backed up with a transparent injection molded back to prevent damage from pool cues.

Advertiser: Löwenbrau Beer
Producer: Process Displays Inc.,
New Berlin, WI

This handsome back-bar display allowed field distributor personnel to secure dominant locations that informed the consumer of the product's availability. The internally illuminated unit used injection molding, rotational molding, and screen printing.

Advertiser: Corona Beer (Barton)
Producer: Visual Marketing Inc., Chicago
Designer: Don Buck

Corona's impact on the market is due, in part, to its bottle, clear, long-necked, with a silk-screened label. To take advantage of the impact of the package, a giant replica, 3' in height, was created to make an excellent point of purchase piece. The bottle was vacuum formed in clear PETG material, with a distorted silk screen label, bottle cap, and beer color. A 10-watt bulb against a silver reflective background created subtle illumination. All it takes for installation is a nail or screw in the wall and a nearby electrical outlet.

Advertiser: Pepsi-Cola Co.
Producer: Thomas A. Schutz Co., Inc.,
                  Morton Grove, IL
Designer: Raymond M. Mikolay

The truck design was developed not only to capture immediate attention by its size and prominent identification, but also to provide a large stable surface, either 8' or 12' in length, from which to merchandise large quantities of Pepsi 12 or 24 packs. The cab was rotationally cast in linear low polyethylene, giving it a strong resilient finish which could be decorated with labels. The truck beds were designed for quick simple assembly. The board used was finished with a melamine laminate and T-molding for durability. The unit could easily be disassembled, moved to another store, and quickly reassembled.

Advertiser: New England Apple Products
                  Co.
Producer: RTC Industries, Inc., Chicago

This floor display holds up to 3 cases of product, keeping the beverages cold for up to 24 hours. With a heavy gauge fiber drain and injection molded plastic bin, the unit is designed to promote sales of cold beverages in convenience stores and other retail outlets.

Advertiser: A & W Beverages Inc.
Producer: Anglo Affiliated Co., New York

Highlighting this massive end-aisle display is a 48" inflated root beer mug, designed to pick up the theme of the combination of root beer and ice cream as a summer treat.

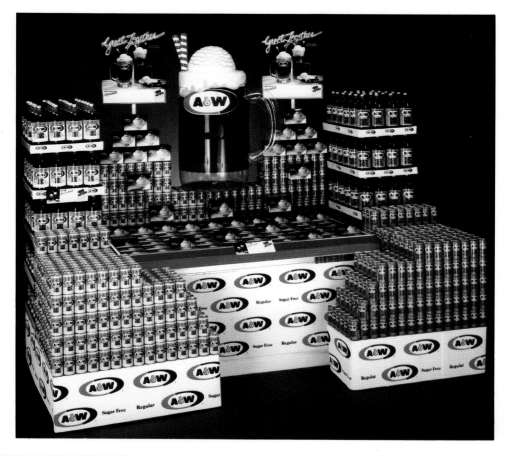

Advertiser: Coca-Cola
Producer: RTC Industries, Inc., Chicago

The first all plastic permanent display in the soft drink industry can be utilized in drug stores and service stations as well as in supermarkets. It can hold 250 2-liter bottles, and can be used on an end aisle. A chrome-plated wire bin can convert one of the flat shelves into a dump bin for special promotional uses. The molded, all-plastic, four-sided embossed header has channels to hold card inserts for promotional tie-ins.

Advertiser: Baron von Scheuter (James Beam Distilling Co.)

Producer: Patrick H. Joyce & Associates, Des Plaines, IL

This unusual kit was issued to help introduce a new line. The cut-out figure was life size, and was supported by the two die-cut, wind-activated mobiles.

Advertiser: Sun Country Wine Cooler (Canandaigua Wines)
Producer: Lawless Display, North Tonawanda, NY
Designer: Jim Southwell

This colorful stack header calls attention to a mass display of the product. The back panel is inter-changeable so the unit can be customized for various promotions.

Advertiser: James B. Beam Distilling Co.
Producer: Creative Displays Inc., Chicago

A Christmas promotion involved single hanging pieces, as well as a mobile, plus stack toppers and shelf talkers.

Advertiser: James B. Beam Distilling Co.
Producer: Trenmark, La Mirada, CA

This unit can sit on a counter or on top of a stack of cases of product. The limited edition model truck ties in with the theme of the promotion.

Advertiser: E & J Brandy (Gallo Winery)
Producer: Tom R. Hoven Associates, Fremont, CA

This end-aisle display uses cases of the product, surmounted by a dignified and attractive hanging identification sign made of polyurethane. Corrugated woodgrain was used on the posts and the cross bar.

Advertiser: E & J Brandy (Gallo Winery)
Producer: Tom R. Hoven Associates, Fremont, CA

This stack topper, designed for end-aisle showings, had a corrugated header and an etched mirror tray from Beeco.

Advertiser: Jose Cuervo Tequila
Producer: Einson Freeman, New York

This free-standing display was designed to establish a long-term, in-store display for the product during the summer months, as well as to gain grocery distribution. The large size—8 x 1 x 12'—and unusual shape encourage end-aisle use. Room was left to stock related products, such as margarita mix, limes, salt, glasses, and so on. In addition to the main display, four free-standing cactus plants were included in the display kit, to provide additional display opportunities at store entry and other strategic locations.

Advertiser: Miller Brewing Co.
Producer: Wetzel Brothers Inc., Milwaukee
Designer: Susan Burdett

To introduce a new product, this colorful tropical display used bright palm trees and stuffed animals, along with case displays.

Advertiser: Fletcher & Oakes (Jim Beam)
Producer: RTC Industries, Inc., Chicago

A pole display, with an unusually-shaped top, suggests the bottle that is on display. The shelves rotate freely for complete sell-through and ease of restacking. The checkerboard pattern in the four-packs is picked up in the base.

Advertiser: Sun Country Wine Cooler
(Canandaigua Wines)
Producer: Lawless Display, North
Tonawanda, NY
Designer: Robert Dye

This three-dimensional cardboard
sculpture, printed on two sides,
encourages mass displays of the
product, and encourages retailers
to carry large quantities.

Advertiser: Fletcher & Oakes
Producer: Creative Displays Inc., Chicago

The background for stack displays of cartons utilized a standard base with changeable toppers. The one-piece display unfolds to provide continuous selling message as the product sells down.

Advertiser: DeKuyper (Jim Beam)
Producer: RTC Industries, Inc., Chicago

Ten different flavors are merchandised in a streamlined, space-efficient display. The unit, triangular in shape, takes less than 4 sq. ft. of floor space. The shelving is injection molded and the header is vacuum formed.

Advertiser: DeKuyper (James Beam Distilling Co.)
Producer: Patrick H. Joyce & Associates, Des Plaines, IL

This back bar piece holds four of the 38 flavors in the product line, permitting the retailer to select local or regional preferences.

Advertiser: Hennessy (Schieffelin & Co.)
Producer: Ettinger Displays Inc., Jericho, NY
Designer: Judd A. Ettinger

Designed for back bar use, this unit is hand beveled to project the high end image the client wishes to promote. The angled mirrors multiply the impact of the display, which exemplifies elegance.

Advertiser: Beefeater Gin & Tonic (Buckingham Wine Co.)
Producer: RTC Industries, Inc., Chicago

The innovative bottle-shaped display is consistent with the distinctive Beefeater image. Large header allows the entire product label to be recreated larger-than-life. The rotating three-tier vacuum-formed merchandise platform provides total visibility to a full case of the new pre-mix cocktails.

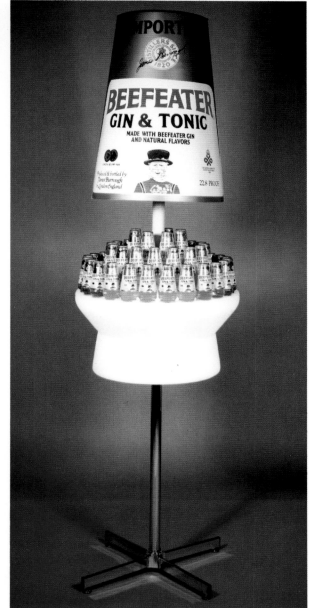

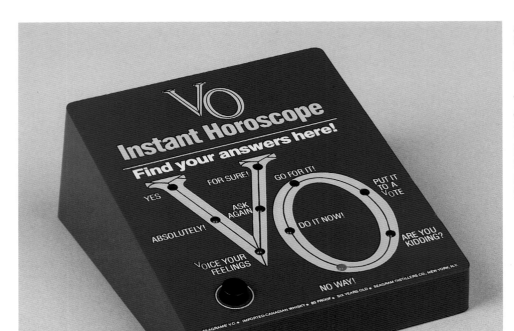

Advertiser: Joseph E. Seagram
Producer: Data Display Systems,
              Philadelphia
Designer: Bob Levitt

This attention-getting display sits on the bar and amuses customers and bartender alike. Ask a question, push the button, and the lights will flash at random for 10 to 15 seconds, before stopping on one of the 10 LEDs.

Advertiser: Joseph E. Seagram
Producer: Data Display Systems,
              Philadelphia
Designer: Bob Levitt

Once each minute, the light goes on for 5 seconds in this dignified back bar display. The molded plastic base, decorated with decals, holds the single battery and the timer which allows it to run for over four months continuously.

Advertiser: Joseph E. Seagram
Producer: Data Display Systems, Philadelphia
Designer: Bob Levitt

The message glows brightly and colorfully when written on this message board, illuminated by a high-brightness fluorescent tube in the molded base. The permanent message is silkscreened on the clear acrylic.

Advertiser: V O Canadian Whiskey (Seagram)
Producer: Visual Marketing Inc., Chicago
Designer: Dennis Nielsen

Basketball was the theme of this promotion, which covered the end of the season and the excitement of the NCAA tournament. The off-premise display consisted of a two-thirds size backboard, with the VO logo, a hoop and net. A 7" imprinted nerf basketball permitted customers to have fun. It was also offered as a self-liquidating premium. For on-premise use, a miniature hoop was developed to sit on the neck of a VO bottle which was set in a smoked acrylic holder. It was designed as a tip collector with the theme "nice tip in." An incentive program offered a trip to the Final Four tournament to the four distributors with the best achievement.

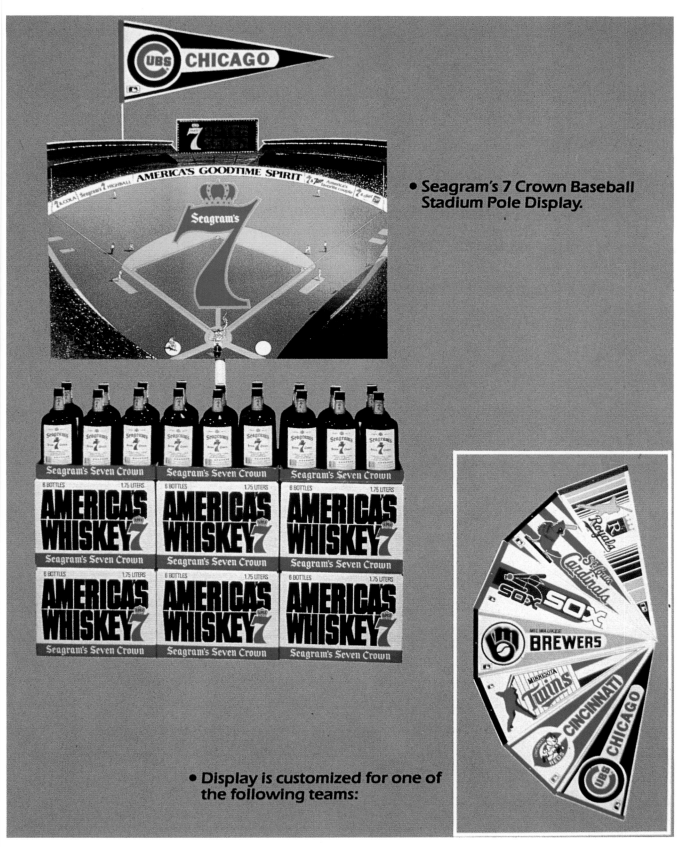

• Seagram's 7 Crown Baseball Stadium Pole Display.

• Display is customized for one of the following teams:

Advertiser:	7 Crown (Seagram)
Producer:	Visual Marketing Inc., Chicago
Designer:	Dennis Nielsen

It's baseball time, and time for a seasonal promotion. Highlight of the display, planned for mounting above a stack of cases of the product, was a generic baseball stadium, on which was superimposed a big red "7" for identification. Drink recipes using 7 Crown were printed as billboards on the stadium walls, and the pennant of a particular team, chosen by the retailer, was attached above the display.

Advertiser: Dribeck Importers
Producer: Brinker Displays,
East Orange, NJ

Dribeck introduced the first German low calorie beer to the United States using this corrugated gift set. It was distributed to liquor stores, supermarkets, bars, and restaurants.

Advertiser: Dewar's Scotch (Schenley Industries)
Producer: Brinker Displays,
East Orange, NJ

This pole-topper display introduced Dewar's year-long celebration of its taste/quality award at the Edinborough Exposition. It included a sweepstakes open to the public.

Advertiser: Canadian Hunter (Seagram)
Producer: Visual Marketing Inc., Chicago
Designer: Dennis Nielsen

This relatively new product had to make its way entirely through its impact at the point of sale, since it was being given no advertising support. The campaign was built around a series of fine arts prints using outdoor settings. The display, using the print framed in oak, with plexiglass for protection, is supplied with pole and foot for off-premise use, while in on-premise locations, it is hung on the wall. After the promotion, the framed print can be removed and used as a gift. A distributor incentive program was developed based on sales, size distribution and display activity, with the winner receiving the original oil painting. Signed and numbered prints were available for distributor sales incentive programs.

Advertiser: Smirnoff Vodka
Producer: Einson Freeman, New York

The last in a series of four promotions, this attracted attention with its tongue-in-cheek offers, like a sable fur coat "for $85,000 and three proofs of purchase." The display promoted three classic drinks: a screwdriver, a bloody mary, and a martini.

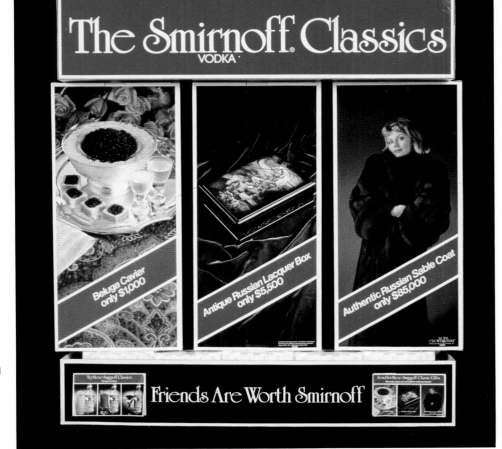

In good company for the holidays

Advertiser: Irish Mist (Hiram Walker)
Producer: The Howard Marlboro Group, New York

Motion in the feature panel attracted the consumer's eye to the product. The display could be used as a pole topper or, as shown, with a bin of product.

Advertiser: Ernest & Julio Gallo Winery
Producer: Data Display Systems, Philadelphia
Designer: Ken Reich

Attention is drawn to this pole-topper by the lights that twinkle on the Christmas tree. A special electronic circuit allows the display to run continuously for 8 weeks on batteries.

POINT-OF-SALE MATERIAL— WHY BOTHER?

H. PIERCE PELOUZE III
Vice President—Promotion
Campbell Soup Company
CAMDEN, NJ

There is often considerable debate, in fact, disagreement, regarding many of the functions of today's marketing and selling organizations. At Campbell Soup Company this debate has recently occurred. In 1986, sweeping changes were made to our basic marketing philosophy and sales force structure, and these changes included renewed priority attention to Campbell product in-store advertising and merchandising.

The significance of these changes resulted in a January 26, 1987 feature in *Business Week.* Described as "marketing's new look," the changes in Campbell's marketing operations reflected our awareness of the need to approach our consumers in a new way. Mass marketing will no longer be the only way Campbell will compete in the marketplace. Regional and local marketing, tailoring our advertising and promotional efforts to limited and specific geographical and consumer segments, will reshape our entire marketing thrust. In addition to changing how we advertise and promote, Campbell's selling organization was also changed from a vertical, product distribution orientation (for example, we had separate canned and frozen foods sales forces) to a geographical selling organization with 21 sales regions across the United States responsible for selling all Campbell products.

Under this new organization, our retail grocery store sales personnel are responsible for all in-store merchandising and other selling efforts. We call it "wall-to-wall." Why are we doing this? <u>The war is in the store</u>. With the array of products Campbell sells, with the competition we face across the U.S., and with our new focus on regional and local marketing, Campbell is committed to facing the war in the store. Point-of-sale merchandising is key. Store display and expanded shelf, freezer, or refrigerated space are priority objectives. And, if we are going to communicate key product benefits and obtain the quantity of displays we seek, point-of-sale materials are an important ally of any professional, effective selling effort.

However, we at Campbell do not have a unique perspective. The October 1987 issue of *Promote* highlighted the growth of the point-of-purchase advertising industry. Double digit growth for the past several years is evident. The burgeoning interest in custom regional, local and key account marketing is indeed exploding in this area.

To give you an idea of the immensity of point-of-purchase advertising spending, note that billions of dollars are involved. In 1986, the Point-of-Purchase Advertising Institute (known as POPAI), the association of the industry, estimated that $10.8 billion were spent on p-o-p displays and materials. For 1987 its projection was $12.6 billion, up 16.6 percent! This is big, big business, over twice the size of Campbell Soup Company, and reflects the major importance companies in many industries across the U.S. have given to the in-store, point-of-purchase advertising environment.

At Campbell, we obviously are interested in this study, because it helps us define our in-store selling strategies and priorities. Let's examine two big Campbell categories: frozen dinners and entrees, and soups. In the case of frozen foods, you'll note that in-store decision accounts for 81 percent of the purchases. This is well above the previously mentioned figure of 66.1 percent. Thus, our retail personnel, whose products include the Swanson and Le Menu brands, must give in-store display and other forms of in-store advertising exposure a high priority. And, look at soups at 73 percent. Again, it's above the average, and again, a signal to give Campbell's soups in-store merchandising considerable attention to gain our share of these impulse purchases.

The war in the store not only generates significant competition for various forms of permanent and promotional display and other point-of-purchase advertising materials, but this battleground has likewise fostered a proliferation of in-store media, also vying for those consumer in-store impulse decisions. We now have messages staring at shoppers as they wheel down the aisles. Some go with you, as shopping cart ads do.

Other messages lie in waiting over the aisle until the customer needs to doublecheck just what's in a particular aisle. And, when he or she does, just before picking something off the shelf, there's a product message and visual that's certainly more memorable than a TV commercial viewed last night.

As another exmaple, there is now a permanent shelf sign, guaranteed to be with the correct product and acting as a flag to grab the consumer's attention, as he or she travels down the aisle. These are only several of a growing list of in-store advertising services that again underscore the present and future importance of in-store impulse decisions and in-store product presence.

Point-of-sale material—why bother? The answer is clear; given the extremely high percentage of in-store impulse purchase decisions, attention to and development of professional in-store P-O-P advertising programs is needed to increase one's share of those well-defined impulse purchases.

Advertiser: Walls Ice Cream
Producer: Lintas Kuala Lumpur, Malaysia
Designer: Albert Choo

A variety of hanging mobiles promote the exotic flavors, including yam, sweet corn, thunder jet and chocodile, of a new line of ice cream products.

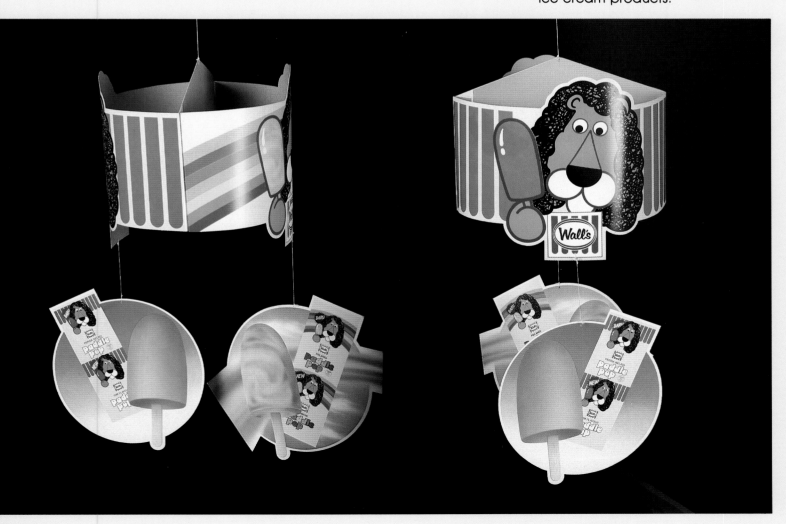

Advertiser: Walls Ice Cream
Producer: Lintas Kuala Lumpur, Malaysia
Designer: Albert Choo

A variety of hanging mobiles promote the exotic flavors, including yam, sweet corn, thunder jet and chocodile, of a new line of ice cream products.

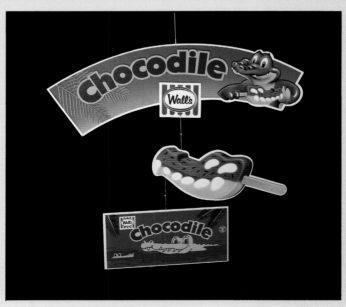

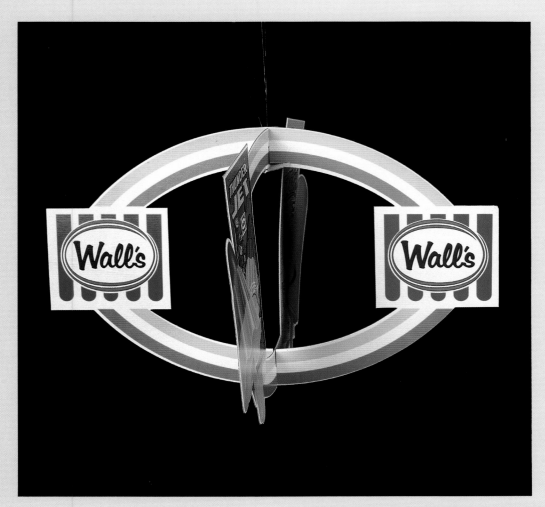

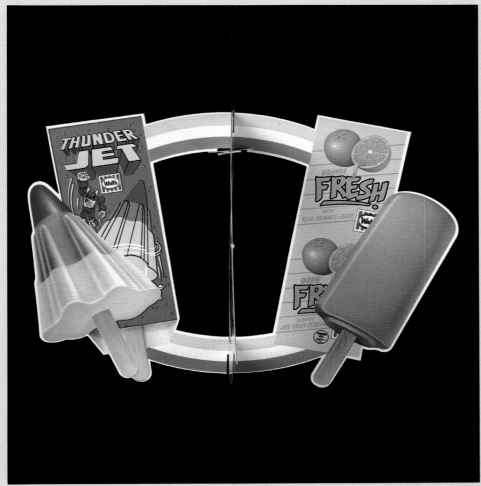

Advertiser: Produce Partners (Libby)
Producer: RTC Industries, Inc., Chicago

This display features five vacuum-formed shelves that can hold 20 cases of the product. The large base, along with two upright supports which fasten to the back of the shelves, adds durability and gives the display a permanent look. It can bring produce-related merchandise into the produce department. The header can be easily changed.

Advertiser: Henri Nestle (Nestle Foods Corp.)
Producer: Creative Displays Inc., Chicago

This counter display, holding four dozen bags of chocolate and keeping them upright, picks up the design of the label to use in the sign. Fits on counter or shelf.

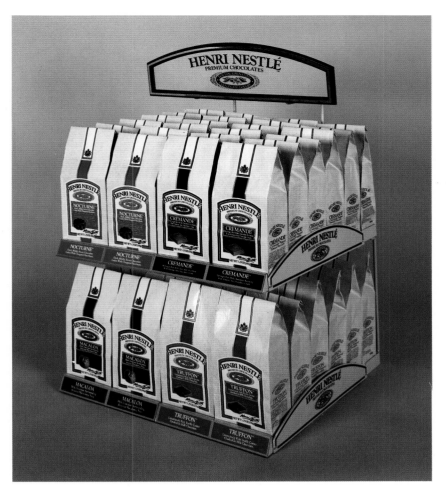

Advertiser: Finley Ltd. (Superior Coffee and Foods)
Producer: Creative Displays Inc., Chicago

This organizer creates an entire department, with room for many varieties of coffee, literature and grinder, all in one unit. Its patented construction holds full facings of bags in an upright position. The drawer-type assembly pulls forward for easy restocking.

Advertiser: Ziploc (Dow Chemical Co.)
Producer: The Acorn Group, Chicago

This prepacked floor stand supported the Young Astronaut program in a back-to-school promotion that offered the customer a premium and provided the retailer with an attention-getting display in less than 4 square feet of floor space.

Advertiser: Schwinn Enterprises
Producer: Process Displays Inc., New Berlin, WI

This striking bi-plane, of screen printed 22 pt coated tag stock and 3/16" foam core, was designed to gain more consumer awareness within the grocery store and create more impulse purchasing. Budget costs were in the $15 to $25 range.

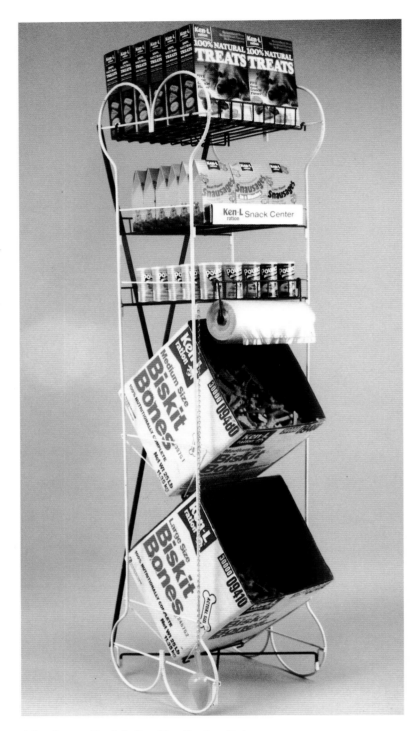

Advertiser: Ken-L Ration (The Quaker Oats Co.)

Producer: Creative Displays Inc., Chicago

This bone-shaped wire unit ships flat and is easy to assemble. In addition to the packages on the three shelves, it holds two cartons of bulk-packed product at an easy to reach angle. A scoop and a roll of plastic bags makes it simple for the customer to make up his order.

Advertiser: Ocean Spray Cranberries

Producer: Display Technologies Inc., Long Island City, NY

This plastic floor stand ships in a small carton, and is easily assembled into a self-standing, attractive display. It moves the product from the gondola shelf to a position of high visibility.

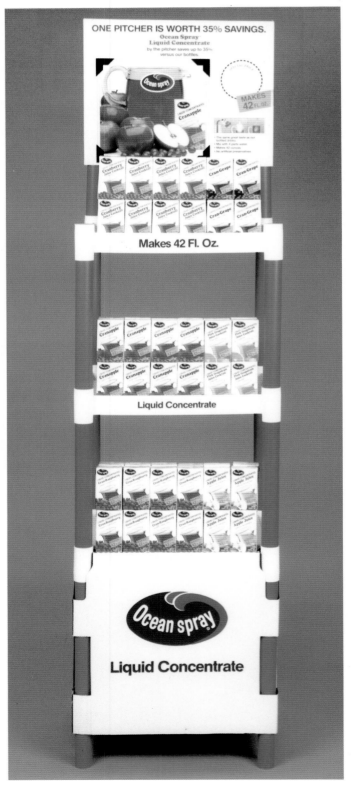

Advertiser: Cap'n Crunch (The Quaker Oats Co.)

Producer: Creative Displays Inc., Chicago

In support of a "Free the Cap'n" promotion, this pole display was highlighted by flashing lights and a phone hotline for those who wanted to rescue the missing character. A taped message delivers a story about finding the cartoon celebrity when a consumer picks up the phone. A Spanish tape was provided for ethnic markets.

Advertiser: Hormel Foods
Producer: RTC Industries, Inc., Chicago

This display occupies less than 5½ sq. ft. of space, and holds over 100 pounds of product, with injection-molded dividers and see-through fences to organize the packages.

A large header and the side panels have plenty of room for product information. In the initial use of this unit, the top shelf incorporates a Microwave Sweepstakes program, with room for entry blanks, a deposit box, and an actual microwave unit.

Advertiser: Uncle Ben's Inc.
Producer: Creative Displays Inc., Chicago

This patented pallet pack offers great visibility and easy access in a prebuilt display. It eliminates store labor by simply moving the entire pallet onto the store floor, where you remove the outer corrugated wrap and set up the header.

Advertiser: Equal (G.D. Searle & Co.
Producer: Creative Displays Inc., Chicago

This shelf extender takes little room but gives plenty of exposure, both for the brand name on the front of the unit, and through almost complete exposure of the package face. The clamp is adjustable so that the product can be vertical even if the price rail is angled.

Advertiser: Lever Brothers
Producer: Lintas Kuala Lumpur, Malaysia
Designer: Albert Choo

This mobile, intended to support the use of Planta Soft Margarine for Chinese New Year baking, comes assembled but ships flat. Simply pushing the edges of the display brings it out to three dimensions.

Advertiser: Dreyer's Ice Cream
Producer: Trenmark, La Mirada, CA
Designer: Joe Demaine

This hanging unit, that jointly promoted two different brands, shipped flat, and was easily transformed into its three-dimensional state.

Advertiser: Rice-A-Roni (The Quaker Oats Co.)

Producer: Creative Displays Inc., Chicago

A cardboard floorstand, picking up the theme of both the advertising and the packaging, brings the feeling of a San Francisco cable car to the display, offering lots of room for product.

ONE OF THE GREAT CHALLENGES

For many years the Point-of-Purchase Advertising Institute, more familiarly known as "Popeye," because of its initials POPAI, has been calling attention to outstanding displays through an annual awards program. Participation in it is wide, from personal experience as a judge, I know that great effort is made to maintain the integrity of the competition. As a result, being named an OMA winner gives great satisfaction to the designer, to the producer, and to the advertiser who were involved in an award winner.

The categories into which this book is divided is patterned after those set up for the most recent OMA competition, so it is consistent with and helps to support this major force of recognition within the industry.

But I am somewhat puzzled by the conglomeration of this category, wondering what the three sub-categories—Tobacco and Tobacco Products; Candy, Gum, Mints; Snack (including chips, popcorn, pretzels, etc.)—have in common   so that their point-of-purchase displays should be judged against each other. The most rational explanation that comes to mind is that these three product categories are all sold through a variety of outlets and that they are almost entirely an impulse purchase, and thus, more likely to be influenced by advertising at the point of sale.

Another thought occurred to me as I worked on this chapter, and that is that I do not foresee an easy time ahead, in the next decade or so, for those involved in the promotion of tobacco products. This is a difficult commodity to promote even today, what with prohibitions on using television, limitations on sales to minors, requirements for including health warnings, and the contradictions involved in making smoking attractive to those who already smoke without making it equally attractive to young people who are not already smoking.

These constrictions and limitations seem bound to increase as the pressures against smoking get greater . Anti-smoking forces are continuing to harass the industry, with laws creating smoke-free environments in the workplace, in restaurants, in meeting places and in airplanes. Merchandisers and sales promotion people will have to work within this atmosphere. It will become increasingly difficult for them to vigorously promote a brand or a product without arousing increased efforts from the opposition, and giving ammunition to the anti-tobacco forces.

And all of this will happen within what will most likely be a dwindling and increasingly competitive market. The changing situation will demand greater ingenuity and creativity among promotion practitioners. It may be a difficul decade in which to operate, but it should be a most interesting one for those who are less deeply involved.

Advertiser: Sunset Ridge (E.H. Brach & Sons)
Producer: Creative Displays Inc., Chicago

A simple wire stand that ships flat and can be assembled without tools holds a dozen open cartons for a mass display of pick-your-own candies. Shelf strips identify varieties of chocolate.

Advertiser: E.J. Brach & Sons
Producer: Patrick H. Joyce and Associates, Des Plaines, IL

This permanent merchandiser for bagged candies could be installed as a floor stand or a counter display, as well as the traditional pegboard installation. One mold produced all three variations.

Advertiser: The Nestle Company, Inc.
Producer: Henschel-Steinau, Inc.,
Englewood, NJ

This bulk display ties in with Nestle's sponsorship of the restoration of the Statue of Liberty, and offers a related premium to consumers. Its patriotic motif won the cooperation of both supermarket chains and the public.

Advertiser: Peanut Butter Boppers (General Mills)
Producer: Creative Displays Inc., Chicago

A prepacked counter dispenser is designed to stand near the cash register where it can promote impulse sales.

Advertiser: Handi-Snack (Kraft Inc.)
Producer: RTC Industries, Inc., Chicago

Vertical dump bins reduce the floor space needed without reducing product capacity. The durable frame and materials make it look permanent. The snap-in side panels and header add visual excitement and permit changeable graphics for season promotions. Molded-in glides allow the display to be moved easily around the store.

Advertiser: E.J. Brach & Sons
Producer: Chicago Show, Chicago

A counter dispenser for unwrapped candies must distribute a limited number each time, show off the colorful candies, and prevent customers from touching either the candy or the areas which the candy touches while being dispensed.

Advertiser: E.J. Brach & Sons
Producer: Patrick H. Joyce and Associates,
Des Plaines, IL

The attached chalkboard permits
the retailer to include his own price
offer or other special message.

Advertiser: Russell Stover Candies Inc.
Producer: RTC Industries, Inc., Chicago

This rotating five-shelf display holds 20 to 30 cases of product in a space only 20" in diameter. Molded shelves are angled to feed product to the front. The unit has created a permanent merchandise center in both stores which carry the company's premium line of chocolates, and has gained access to retailers who do not handle the full line.

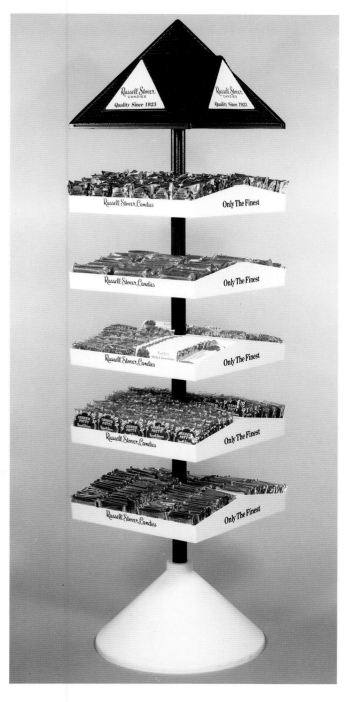

Advertiser: New Trail Granola Bar (Hershey Chocolate Co.)
Producer: Henschel-Steinau, Inc., Englewood, NJ

This display ships almost flat, and is easily assembled by snapping the side supports into the four trays. Used to introduce a new product, the lightweight unit holds four full cartons of the product.

Advertiser: Fedora Candy
Producer: Deijon Inc., Carlstadt, NJ
Designer: Vince Gambello

Constructed of wood and clear acrylic plastic, this merchandiser creates a permanent off-shelf home for this brand. A gravity feed feature allows products to feed forward as they are removed from the display, keeping the product neat and organized during the sell-through.

Advertiser: Benson and Hedges
Producer: Gallaher Limited, Northolt, Middlesex, England

This large kiosk, is designed for free standing in high traffic areas.

Advertiser: O'Grady's Potato Chips (Frito-Lay Inc.)
Producer: Pioneer Balloon Co., Wichita, KS

Easily inflatable package replica balloons were used to call attention to a contest that would introduce a new product. To simplify distribution, packets included the balloon, an instruction clip, a patented closure clip, a piece of double-stick tape, and a hand inflator. The balloons were also tied to Suzuki 4x4s, the grand prize of the contest, which were parked outside of stadiums before National Football League games.

Advertiser: Silk Cut
Producer: Gallaher Limited, Northolt,
                 Middlesex, England

These kiosks, made up of the same
basic elements, can be adjusted to
fit the specific location.

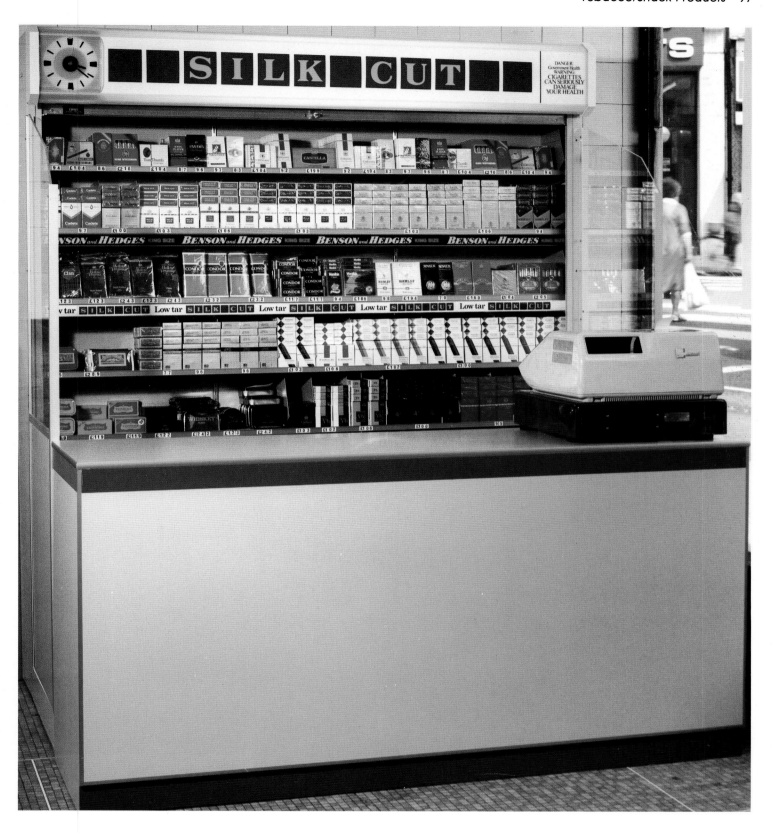

Advertiser: Philip Morris USA
Producer: Process Displays Inc.,
New Berlin, WI

The hanging, illuminated sign served multiple purposes. It promoted brand awreness; its open/closed feature informed the consumer; it also served as a night light when the store was closed. It is made of injection-molded styrene with screen-printed acrylic. Designed for three-year use, its cost is in the $25-$50 range.

Advertiser: RJR Sales Company
Producer: RTC Industries, Inc., Chicago

The spring-loaded racks in this unit always present the full face of all the cigarette packs. The units can be combined to give in-line arrangements, as well as for end-aisle, free standing, or check-out merchandising. Vacuum formed headers offer additional promotional space.

Advertiser: Kool Cigarettes
Producer: Chicago Show, Chicago

This group of advertising signs helps
the retailer by providing useful
information, such as the date, the
time, pricing, and hours of business.
The neutral frames fit any location,
and set off the colorful inserts. They
can be changed from one brand to
another by simply replacing the
inserts, which are held against the
clear covers by polyester foam
backing.

Advertiser: Generic
Producer: Deijon Inc., Carlstadt, NJ/
Design Wire Products Inc.

This wooden merchandiser is designed to put high impulse items near the check-out lines in supermarkets. With shelves on three sides, it can service two check-out counters at one time.

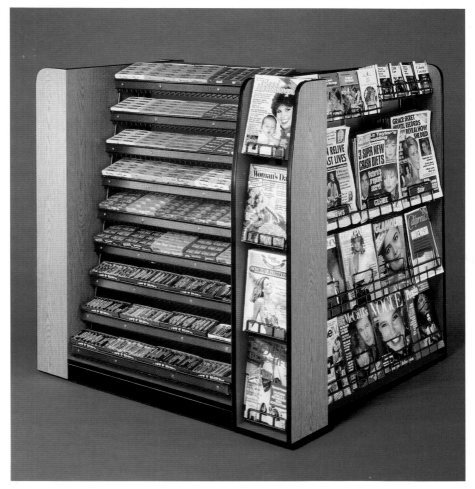

Advertiser: Eckerd Drug Co.
Producer: Deijon Inc., Carlstadt, NJ/
Design Wire Products Inc.

This modular island display offers good visibility to a large number of products. The tilted wire baskets keep the merchandise always available.

THE FUTURE IS BRIGHT FOR DISPLAY

ROBERT C. THORBORG
Manager of Marketing Services
Corning Glass Works
CORNING, NY

Having been involved, one way or another, in the POP environment for the last 25 plus years, I am amazed by the number of changes that have taken place at the retail counter, and more specifically in the retail environment itself.

We have gone from a customer-and-service oriented policy, with its multitude of highly trained retail personnel to aid in decision making, to today's mass appeal, find-and-choose-it approach.

Customers have been indoctrinated that in order to achieve quality at a price they must give up some of the costly "service" overheads associated with the retail environment. This consists, in part, of minimizing "back room" stock space in order to pile the goods on the retail floor where they can be seen . . . and where customers can serve themselves.

The most notable change, though, is found in the decline of knowledgeable salespeople to assist consumers with their purchases. This was the greatest single factor influencing the POP industry. It gave the display industry the opportunity —indeed the charge—to serve the retail industry, and more importantly, the customer, by providing information needed to make objective decisions in this new open store environment which offered multitudes of similar and competing products.

As the mass retail industry grew and prospered over the past 20 years, the proliferation of operations made it paramount that mass retailers build identities that would consistently bring customers in and, more importantly, create customer loyalty and repeat business. Chain stores, with this image in mind, took lessons from the traditional department stores they competed against, and started to create a corporate image, not on a local basis but rather nationally. The use of manufacturers' logos, which was so prevalent at the start of this industry boom, was replaced by corporate signage, and it became virtually impossible to place a manufacturer's sign in these establishments. The stores evolved from low-price, volume-based, name-brand businesses into one with their own names and images. They often redesigned their stores to reflect this image change. In the process, the POP industry gained new clients by going directly to the retail establishments and aiding in the development of their specific "look," as well as the area of in-house branded merchandise.

These same retailers now face the same issues which helped get them entrenched years ago: tremendous competition for the consumer dollar. In response to these pressures, they are turning to their major suppliers to create programs specifically geared to their retail operations along with the manufacturers' commitments of exclusivity for given time periods. This is being done with both house brands and with name-branded specific sets, open stock items, decorations, etc. Freed under these arrangements from the threat of competitive price undercutting, they are willing to allow more freedom in the use of manufacturers' logos and fixtures to help merchandise the products. Again, the POP industry reaps the benefits through opportunities to develop store-specific displays and promotions.

While I'm not a guru, nor am I endowed with special powers to see into the future, here is what I expect for the POP industry for the next five years or so:

(1) The trend to more retailer-specific displays and promotional packages will gain emphasis at the cost of generic displays. This again will be done to insure that the retail trade has item-specific opportunities to promote without the fear of head-to-head competition from across the street. These items—and the companies producing them—will become partners in the development of these displays, and the POP industry will work with both clients in their development. We have seen this already at our company, where we have designed retail-specific displays and programs for our customers. One such project was the design of fixtures for our open stock Correlle® dinnerware that involved over 20 units and combinations. These different designs were generated to fit individual fixture size requirements, mix of items and special headers or shelf strips to "fit" store environments. This process of selective display programs will continue, and the POP industry will have not only the manufacturer as a client but also the retailer. Due to this change, the order quantities on any one display will, in all likelihood, become smaller, but in the long run you will probably get more fixtures/ displays placed on any given program.

(2) Displays will be designed with packaging in mind and will be coordinated with it. It is my opinion that one of the most vital forms of POP which has not been fully addressed or understood by this industry is the role of packaging in informing the customer of the benefits of the product they are reviewing., In many instances, the package is the only vehicle at the retail counter that carries the manufacturers' messages and is key in providing the necessary inducements to close the sale. In the future, packaging development and the more traditional forms of POP must work as a team in developing the most effective on-the-counter displays. Many companies have combined or are combining the functions of packaging and POP development into one department. I see this trend continuing, enabling us to present a full retail package to the consumer.

(3) More displays will, as stated above, be used for item- or program-specific promotions. Therefore, the displays will be shipped already packed, or along with the ware on pallets. Gone are the days when generic displays were shipped to distributors in the hope that they would at least get to the retail store if not to the counter. With cost a major issue, a concerted effort is being made to ensure complete use of all display materials in the correct retail environment. Drop shipment direct to the retailer will continue to grow, and the use of fulfill-ment operations will flourish.

In summary, then, the entire industry will enjoy substantial growth in meeting retailers' needs in providing item/promotion-specific programs. However, to enjoy this projection, one must be on the leading edge. As more and more retailers realize the dollar return potential of point-of-purchase advertising, versus any other type of promotional vehicle, more money will be directed toward reaching the consumer through the retail counter.

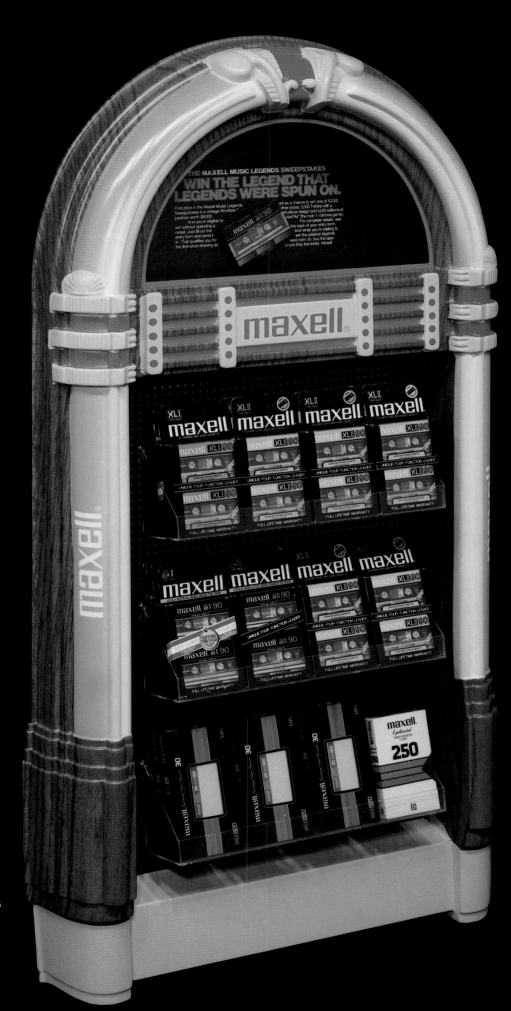

Advertiser: Maxell America
Producer: The Syn-Comm Group Inc.,
New York
Designer: Kenneth Curtis

Designed to tie in with a promotion built around themes of the 1950s, the unit is a full-sized replica of a jukebox of that period. The graphics were silkscreened onto plastic, with allowances made to compensate for the distortion of thermoforming. The shell was then attached to a metal frame, with pegboard and signs added later.

Advertiser: Generic
Producer: Deijon Inc., Carlstadt, NJ
Designer: Vince Gambello

This system is composed of shelf plates which fit into standard pegboard. Effective for displaying video cassettes, compact discs, and paperback books, it holds the product at a 45 degree angle.

Advertiser: Supervideo
Producer: Benchmarc Display Inc., Prospect Heights, IL

This unusual fixture displays nearly 300 mini-posters, each with a description and code number. Punching the number on any of the four key-pad stations brings an immediate report on whether that title is in stock or not. The display speeds up selection and reduces shoppers' disappointment with out-of-stock titles.

Advertiser: 3M
Producer: RTC Industries, Inc., Chicago

Merchandising blank recording tape, both audio and video, this unit uses strong injection-molded rotors, which stack to give infinite flexibility and fully utilizes the entire merchandising area. Bold graphics at the top and bottom of the display help create a strong selling theme. Optional snap-on pockets hold literature.

Advertiser: Waldenbooks
Producer: The Syn-Comm Group Inc., New York
Designer: Kenneth Curtis

This unit was designed to emphasize the product, leaving the structure almost invisible. Using variable vertical spacers, the unit can accommodate audio, video, or CD products.

Advertiser: Wegmans Supermarkets
Producer: Deijon Inc., Carlstadt, NJ
Designer: Vince Gambello

The merchandising system utilized in this unit is made of clear injection molded plastic pieces that adjust to form individual pockets of the exact sizes needed, thus achieving maximum utilization of the space. Slatwall is used on the ends and pegboard on the sides.

Advertiser: Kartes Video Communications
Producer: Deijon Inc., Carlstadt, NJ
Designer: Wolf Dietrich Hannecke

The revolving unit provides easy customer access. It allows full facing and spine exposure for 90 video cassettes. High product visibility enables inventory gaps to be spotted quickly, making restocking easy.

Advertiser: Coleco
Producer: Deijon Inc., Carlstadt, NJ
Designer: Wolf Dietrich Hannecke

This unit holds 36 video games in a minimal amount of space. The adjustable tube allows for merchandising of different sizes of product.

Advertiser: Nightingale-Conant Corp.
Producer: Creative Displays Inc., Chicago

This compact display gains additional off-shelf distribution, even in crowded stores.

Advertiser: Coleco
Producer: Deijon Inc., Carlstadt, NJ
Designer: Wolf Dietrich Hannecke

This 72 pocket freestanding display has a clear circular locking shield to permit product visibility while protecting against pilferage.

Advertiser: Generic
Producer: Deijon Inc., Carlstadt, NJ
Designer: Vince Gambello

This free-standing, four-sided island unit can merchandise an assortment of entertainment/leisure items, including compact discs, software, books, and video and audio products.

Advertiser: View-Master Ideal Group Inc.
Producer: Creative Displays Inc., Chicago

To promote a video product, what could be more appropriate than a permanent display that includes a full-color video screen and an automatically rewound video player?

Advertiser: Nightingale-Conant Corp.
Producer: Creative Displays Inc., Chicago

This compact, economical display enhances brand recognition in a space-saving rotating column. Four dozen cassettes can be kept available. The unit was designed to cost substantially less than an injection-molded plastic display.

Advertiser: Atari (Warner Communications)
Producer: Trenmark, La Mirada, CA

When the customer picks up the receiver of the central telephone, a taped message, supported by six backlit instructional panels that light up sequentially, outlines the product benefits. The unit divides into a counter unit and a wall-hung unit, while the side shelves are removable and adjustable.

Advertiser: Fisher-Price
Producer: David Brace Displays, Lancaster, NY

An actual camera mounted in the display went into action on the push of a button, showing the customer himself in the video screen. Clear sheets of plexiglass acted as a theft deterrent.

Advertiser: Sony Corp.
Producer: Ledan Inc., New York

The complete portable video pack contains its own rechargeable power pack which permits it to be used anywhere. Immediate playback permits on-the-spot critiquing. For traveling, it folds down and is completely waterproof.

Advertiser: General Electric Co.
Producer: Harbor Industries, Grand Haven, MI
Designer: Jeff Bumbera

An exciting new product demanded an exciting new display. Here the dishwasher is mounted at eye level in a unit that is surmounted by a four-sided, illuminated header. An interactive mechanism, sensitive to touch, explains the dishwashing cycles. Mounted on heavy duty casters, the unit is easily moved.

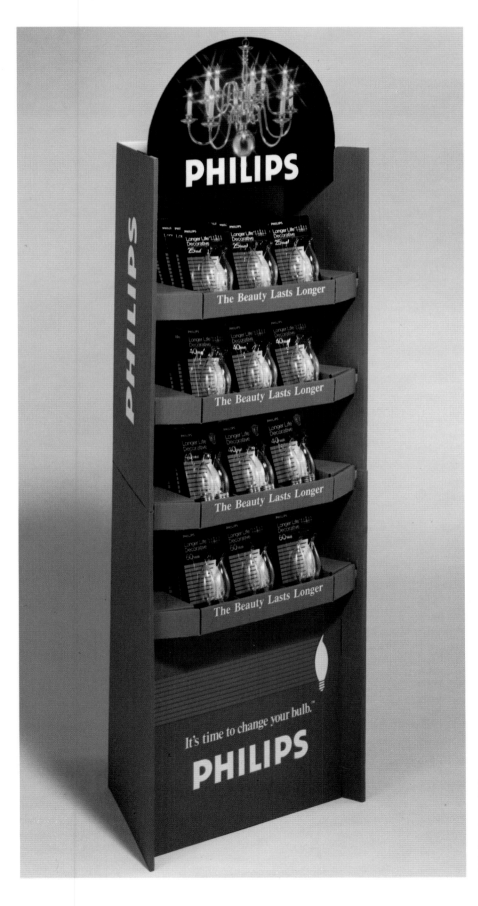

Advertiser: The Philips Lighting Co.
Producer: The Acorn Group, Chicago

This corrugated stand gives a suggestion of the architectural elegance in which these decorative bulbs are used.

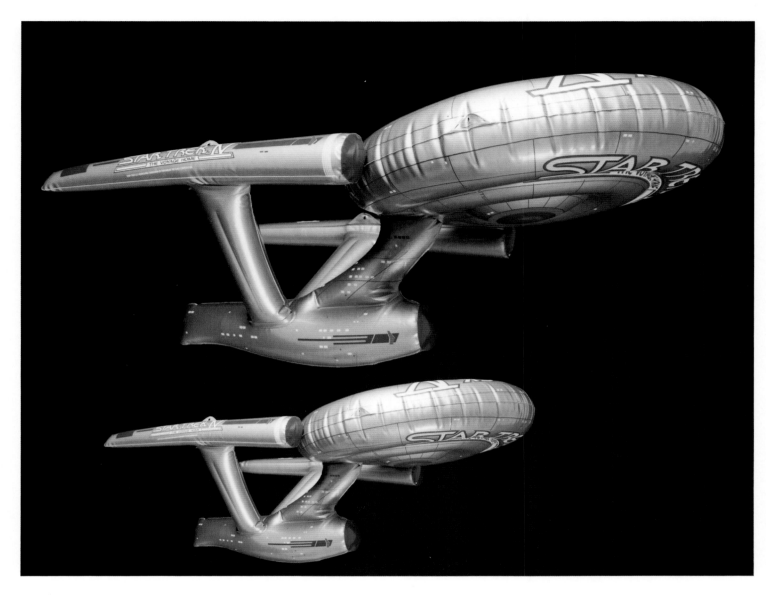

Advertiser: Paramount Pictures Corp.
Producer: Sterling Promotional Corp.,
Great Neck, NY

Inflatable mobile Star Trek replicas came in 29" and 48" sizes to help introduce the release of a series of Star Trek titles on home video.

Advertiser: Philips Lighting Co.
Producer: The Acorn Group, Chicago

This prepack exhibit, of corrugated board, encouraged better lighting for reading and studying, especially appropriate during the back-to-school selling season.

Advertiser: Lifetime Cutlery Corp.
Producer: Ettinger Displays, Inc.,
  Jericho, NY
Designer: Judd A. Ettinger

This attractive unit, of wood and clear plastic, displays the full line and permits easy access to the more popular items.

Advertiser: Cambridge Cleaning System
  (Regina Co.)
Producer: Associated Packaging Inc.,
  West Deptford, NJ
Designer: William Manteufel

This unit replaces a permanent, much more expensive display rack. It ships, knocked down, through the regular mail or UPS, and can be set up quickly. The retailer can display any one of three different models on the same stand, simply by changing the copy card.

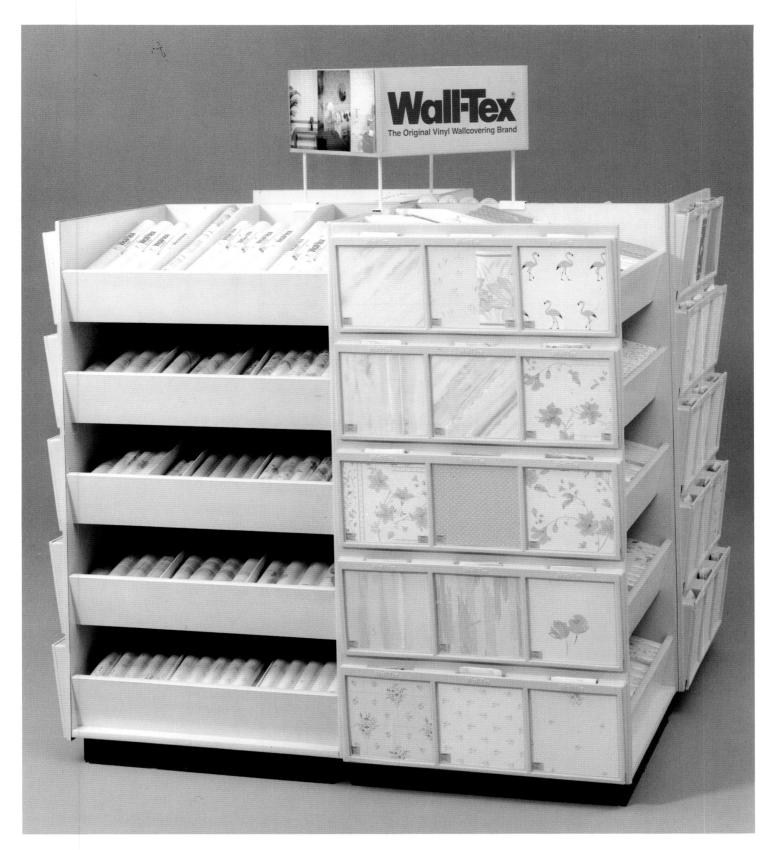

Advertiser: Columbus Coated Fabrics (Borden Inc.)
Producer: The Acorn Group, Chicago

Here is a modular unit that supports a self-service program in outlets that previously sold patterns only from a sample book. The rolls of paper are stored where they are easily reached, while the sample swatches minimize handling. Extra pieces of the swatches are available to take home.

LOOKING AHEAD TO THE '90s

CURTIS K. YOCUM
Manager, Trade Show and Sample Program
American Olean Tile Company
LANSDALE, PA

Eye-catching, educational and useful —these are the watchwords for point-of-purchase displays in the 1990s and beyond. With a growing level of sophistication among consumers, both do-it-yourselfers and professional tradespeople will be demanding more from displays than just pretty pictures.

In addition, the need for displays to meet a variety of price points will continue to grow. There is also likely to be increasing demand for displays that address growing specialty markets; to create custom displays for these niche markets, more companies will probably turn to partnering or joint ventures.

When American Olean Tile Company entered the point-of-purchase arena three years ago with its Ceramic Excitement Center, we had hoped one display could meet the needs of all our retail dealers. The truth was vastly different. And today, we offer more than a half dozen different displays, each aimed at a variety of price points.

We found we had a large number of customers who were unable to make the investment our Ceramic Excitement Center required for a variety of reasons. The price of this top-of-the-line model precluded some dealers from carrying ceramic tile. That certainly wasn't the idea. We wanted to entice people into the business—not keep them out of it!

So over the years, we've developed a number of display varieties including a simple waterfall vision perfect for people, such as builders, who are interested in showing only a few lines of ceramic tile. The basic display shows a limited variety of ceramic tile in a way that's flexible, easy-to-use and allows products to be grouped by function and color. It makes selecting products for new homes a pleasant diversion, not a chore.

In addition to developing the modestly priced waterfall display, we've also increased the range of mid-priced displays and included some custom options. An increasingly popular design is our five-strut satellite display. It takes up very little room and effectively shows every product American Olean manufactures. It also provides retailers with a custom board to mount their own locally stocked items.

Interestingly, we found that the more varieties we offered, the more attractive our top end model became. People perceived it as a real value.

Just as we've discovered that retailers have a need for displays at a variety of price points and options, we've also discovered that the end-user, the customer, has a need for different product information. For example, in the burgeoning do-it-yourself market, homeowners are looking for displays that provide clear, basic educational information. Displays shouldn't be cluttered with too much technical information. An easy-to-follow format of step-by-step information would put the buyer at ease and make him feel confident he can do the work.

Professional installers, on the other hand, are often looking for hard and fast technical information. They generally know the basic differences between products; they don't know why yours works better. It's up to you and your display to tell them. In American Olean's case, ceramic tile installers are interested in what products can be used where. We provide that information on our displays, eliminating any second-guessing.

Over the course of developing these displays, we've also become increasingly involved in joint venture projects to provide custom-tailored displays for specific niche markets. This is likely to become a more frequent occurrence in the future as companies look to expand into specialty markets but with lowered risks.

Hooking up with a retailer or distributor to address a specific market is very attractive. First of all, it increases the likelihood of succeeding with a display. Secondly, it diminishes risk by eliminating the need to develop a large-scale program. Developing displays in conjunction with retailers or distributors may provide in-roads to highly saturated markets or unfamiliar ones. And by sharing the development and costs, both companies benefit and prosper.

The bottom line in creating point-of-purchase displays that work is knowing who you want to reach and what the end-user needs. One display can't be everything to everybody. In addition, whomever your audience is, be sure to discuss products in a language they can relate to.

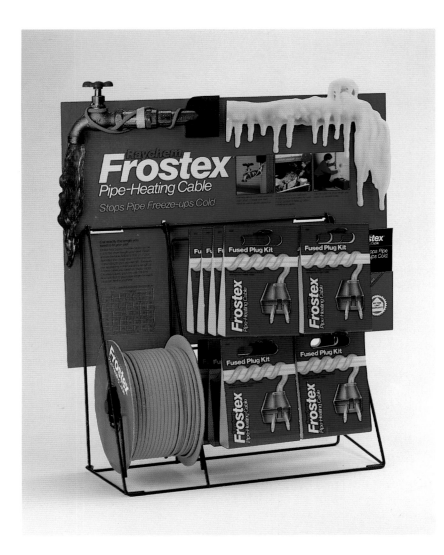

Advertiser: Raychem Corporation
Producer: The Van Noy Group, Torrance, CA

This compact dramatic display sits on a counter and communicates key product benefits. It also acts as a dispenser for the cable.

Advertiser: Markel
Producer: David Brace Displays Inc., Lancaster, NY
Designer: Jeanne Fornes

The black thermo-formed shape featured a metallic gold logo, while the warm red complemented the warm shades of the product photographs.

Advertiser: Haener Stack-King
Producer: Decorr, Div. of Hughes Containers Ltd., Toronto

To demonstrate the uses and features of a new interlocking cement block, the designer developed a promotion card that fits on an actual stack of product, and points out the blocks' key features.

Advertiser: Polycell
Producer: Gallaher Limited, Northolt,
Middlesex, England

This merchandising display holds a
large supply of product, in a
number of sizes, as well as
demonstration samples, instructions,
and product leaflets.

Advertiser: Pratt & Lambert
Producer: David Brace Displays Inc.,
Lancaster, NY

A graphic demonstration, which
permitted the consumer to see for
himself, proved the product
benefits. The dramatic results
helped move product.

Advertiser: Ray O Vac
Producer: The Acorn Group, Chicago

This corrugated floor stand is attractive and compact, and most important of all, it moved product off the retail floor.

Advertiser: Rust-Oleum Corporation
Producer: RTC Industries, Inc., Chicago

A display kit turns an existing gondola into an inexpensive yet effective rust treatment center. An extruded plastic component adheres to the front of the shelf with pressure-sensitive tape. Its upper channel carries individual product identification, while the lower channel serves as an advertising medium. Molded plastic dividers snap into the top of the extrusion to divide the shelves according to product mix. A full-color header completes the customization with brand identifying graphics and advertising.

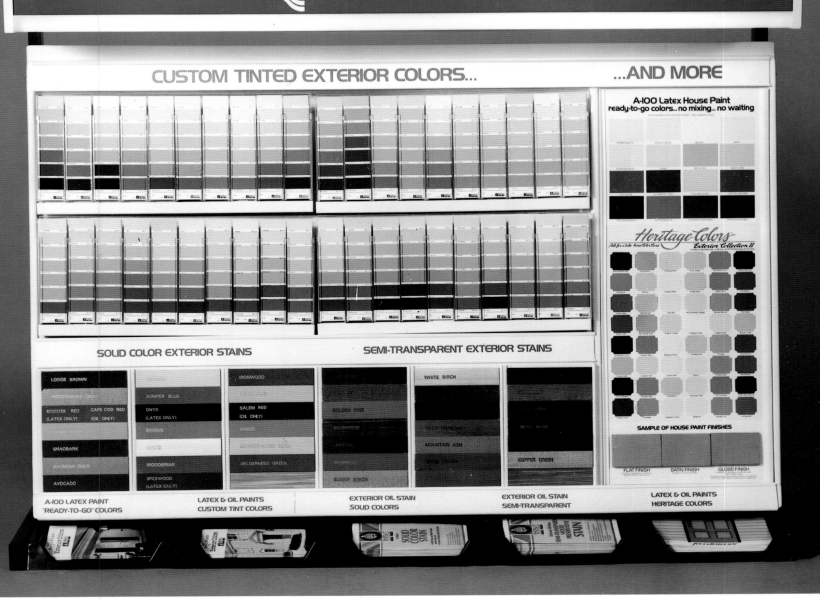

SHERWIN-WILLIAMS EXTERIOR COLORS

CUSTOM TINTED EXTERIOR COLORS... ...AND MORE

SOLID COLOR EXTERIOR STAINS   SEMI-TRANSPARENT EXTERIOR STAINS

A-100 Latex House Paint
ready-to-go colors...no mixing...no waiting

Heritage Colors
Exterior Collection II

SAMPLE OF HOUSE PAINT FINISHES

FLAT FINISH   SATIN FINISH   GLOSS FINISH

LODGE BROWN
WOODSMOKE GRAY
ROOSTER RED   CAPE COD RED
(LATEX ONLY)   (OIL ONLY)
SHAGBARK
HAYMOW GOLD
AVOCADO

JUNIPER BLUE
ONYX
(LATEX ONLY)
BRONZE
WHITE
WOODBRIAR
SPICEWOOD
(LATEX ONLY)

IRONWOOD
DRIFTWOOD
SALEM RED
(OIL ONLY)
EMBER
WILDERNESS GREEN

GOLDEN PINE

WHITE BIRCH

MOUNTAIN ASH

COPPER GREEN

A-100 LATEX PAINT
'READY-TO-GO' COLORS

LATEX & OIL PAINTS
CUSTOM TINT COLORS

EXTERIOR OIL STAIN
SOLID COLORS

EXTERIOR OIL STAIN
SEMI-TRANSPARENT

LATEX & OIL PAINTS
HERITAGE COLORS

Advertiser: Sherwin Williams Inc.
Producer: Patrick H. Joyce and Associates,
Des Plaines, IL

This merchandiser for exterior paint has all the information needed by the consumer to decide exactly what he or she wants, thus cutting down on the salesman's time. There are compartments in which literature can be organized and a built-in lighting fixture adds to the utility of the unit.

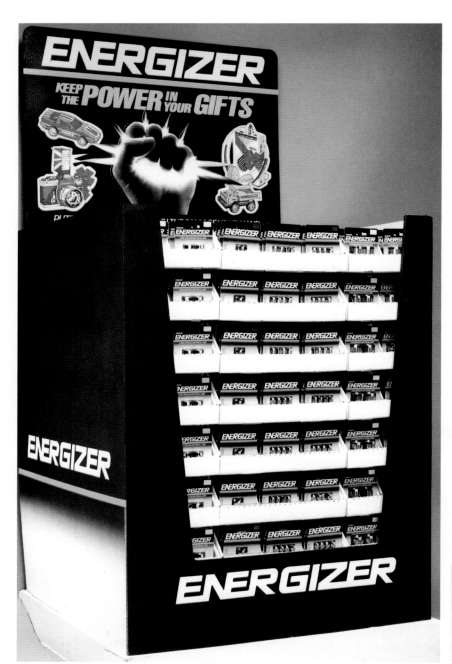

Advertiser: Eveready (Canda) Inc.
Producer: Decorr, Div. of Hughes
Containers Ltd., Toronto

This prepacked pallet is moved in place by hand cart or lift truck and unwrapped for immediate use. The only set-up needed is to activate the motorized backer card.

Advertiser: Panduit Co.
Producer: The Acorn Group, Chicago

Actual samples of the product are mounted to decorated pegboard. The units are designed for use by electrical distributors to make it easy for contractors to develop their orders.

Advertiser: Capital Trading Co.
Producer: Boise Cascade Corp.,
          Sunnyvale, CA
Designer: Robert Marlin

This counter display, with its vacuum molded tray, has high visibility for the product, but inhibits pilfering.

Advertiser: Western Bark Co.
Producer: Boise Cascade Corp.,
          Sunnyvale, CA
Designer: Robert Marlin

This carton served as its own display. It shipped flat and once set up, a poly bag of manure could be added to the package.

Advertiser: Zenith Electronics
Producer: Patrick H. Joyce and Associates, Des Plaines, IL

These signs, of rich, heat-formed black plexiglass, are placed on top of the luxurious television sets they describe, and maintain the image of quality.

Advertiser: Purina Mills Inc.
Producer: The Acorn Group, Chicago

This unit permits farmers to see, touch, and smell actual product samples, and to pick up a folder giving the specifications of each. While it could stand by itself, it was most often used in conjunction with stacks of the product.

SELLING THROUGH INFORMATION

This chapter has about as long and as varied a list of products as any in this book. It includes jewelry; disposables like lighters, pens and razors; photographic equipment; sports equipment; toys, books and games; apparel and footwear; and sewing notions and apparel-making accessories. This wide variety of products has little in common other than the fact that most of them are discretionary products, tending to be luxuries rather than necessities.

In addition, they often involve complicated evaluations and subtle differences between models and brands. Consumers of these products are likely to have questions to be answered. They will want to know whether the product on display has the features and the characteristics that will meet their needs. These are not purchases that customers will make almost off-handedly.

Yet, as is indicated by more than one of the experts who have contributed introductions to chapters in this book, the sales staff available in many retail outlets is changing and is expected to continue to change. There are likely to be fewer salespeople on the floor, and those that remain are likely to be less experienced and less knowledgeable.

This means that, in order to complete a sale, the merchandise must sell itself. Packaging and labeling will contain more information more clearly presented, and it will be supplemented by point-of-purchase displays that inform and instruct, as well as promote. This trend is already under way, and there are examples of it scattered throughout this volume.

There will probably be an increase in self-contained displays, where merchandise is prepacked in a display, with the minimum amount of labor and stock handling required to get it into action. Similar considerations will apply to permanent or semi-permanent fixtures. These will be designed to make it easier for the customer to find the merchandise he or she wants, to select what meets his or her needs, and permit the sale to be completed with only the help of a cashier. At the same time, the fixture will be easier to check for its contents, to determine outages and to refill to capacity, again cutting down on the need for manpower.

Each of the subcategories with the general Personal Products and Accessories area is, of course, different, and these conclusions and predictions will vary from one to the other. But the guiding principle will be clear: in-store displays must—and will—help to minimize the difficulties produced by a shrinking sales force, in numbers as well as in skills.

Advertiser: Mattel Toys
Producer: Process Displays Inc.,
New Berlin, WI

This counter display, featuring Tim Conway, has a working sample of the toy, which changes from one form to another. A battery-powered motor hidden within the display works the toys.

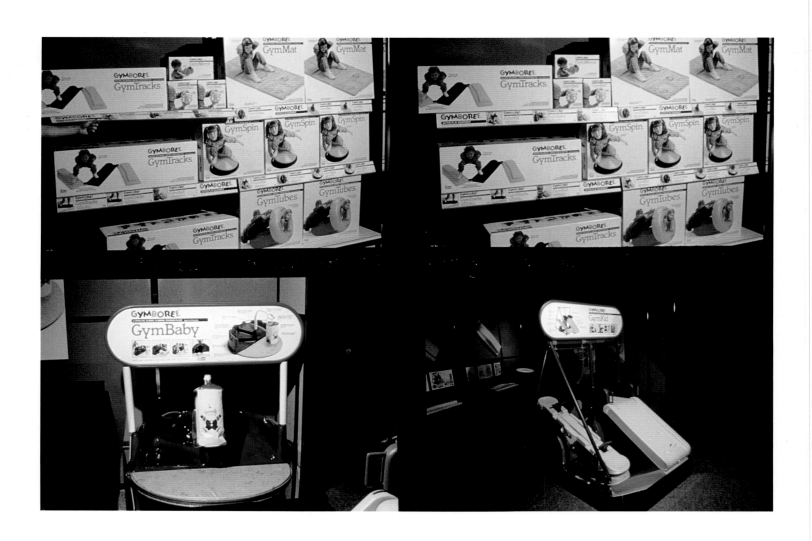

A fairy tale world of Pixietail™ magic!

Advertiser: Mattel Toys
Producer: Process Displays Inc.,
New Berlin, WI

The colorful diorama featured a number of moving parts, activated by an electric motor, which helped to carry out the fairy tale world environment.

Advertiser: Connor Toy Co.
Producer: Thomson-Leeds Co. Inc., New York

A modular sign system was created to attach to the actual product—children's play equipment—when it was on the floor, as well as a shelf sign system.

Advertiser: View-Master Ideal Group Inc.
Producer: Creative Displays Inc., Chicago

Toys that talk and move need to be seen and heard, and this unit, 120v or battery-operated, does this at the touch of a button. The angled backboard concentrates the sound within the unit.

Advertiser: Applause
Producer: United California Display, South Gate, CA
Designer: Jim Ong

This display holds various dolls in a whimsical environment designed to draw the consumer's attention to the product.

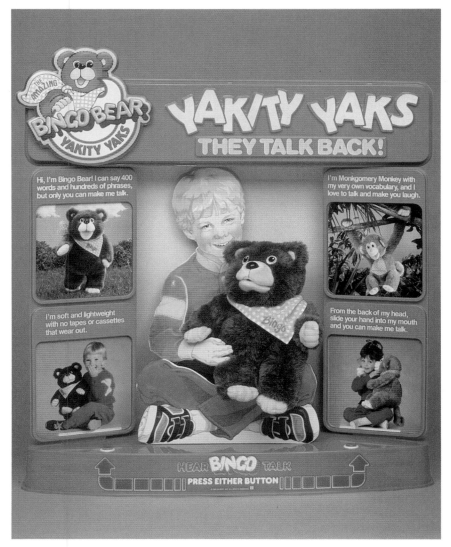

Advertiser: Hasbro Toys
Producer: Thomson-Leeds Co. Inc., New York

Bingo, the talking bear, demonstrates his skill in this display as he sits in the arms of a three-dimensional child. Touching a button starts the sound and the synchronized lips of the toy animal.

Advertiser: Timberland Co.
Producer: Thomson-Leeds Co. Inc., New York

These matching units, of wood veneer slatwall, concentrate attention of the product. Lighted headers, carpeted shelves, and plastic holders, with panels for ad reprints, helps maintain and build the company image.

Advertiser: International Playthings
Producer: Thomson-Leeds Co. Inc., New York

The slotted trays hold various sizes of boxes. The white plastic was selected to fit with the bright colored games and puzzles on display.

Advertiser: Alladin Industries Inc.
Producer: Henschel-Steinau, Inc., Englewood, NJ

The corrugated tower fits in the injection-molded base, and a large 4-color lithographed header tops the display. The lunch boxes hang simply on wooden dowels, making an attractive island display.

Advertiser: Sears, Roebuck & Co.
Producer: Rapid Mounting and Finishing
Co., Chicago

Two elements were developed to support a feature of the month. The first was a three-sided 6' tall floor unit, made of foam core. The other was a hanging sign, also of foam core, with special adjustable wings. both pieces were embossed for added attraction.

Advertiser: Sears, Roebuck & Co.
Producer: Rapid Mounting and Finishing Co., Chicago

An activity center for children, designed to be in the middle of a children's department, not only attracted the kids, but was also an effective selling tool. The unit was 9' tall and 2' square. The silkscreened wood tree had foamboard branches. It incorporated a VCR, a television set, a masonite growth chart and a fun mirror.

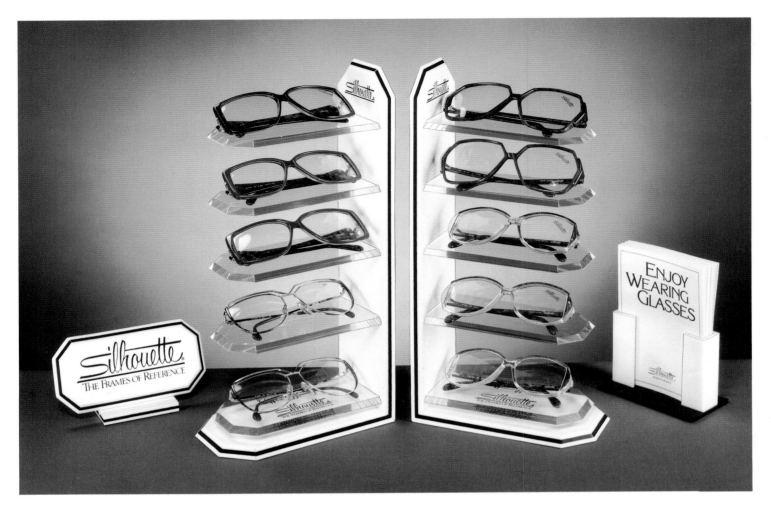

Advertiser: Silhouette Eyewear
Producer: Astra Products Inc., Paterson, NJ
Designer: Thomas Mulvihill

These handsome eyeglass holders are made of laminated and beveled acrylic. The edge-glued shelves were tested to support more than 8 pounds per shelf.

Advertiser: Bausch & Lomb
Producer: Thomson-Leeds Co. Inc., New York

To identify sales locations of Ray-Ban sunglasses, either indoors or outdoors, this sign uses the company's script with a neon effect.

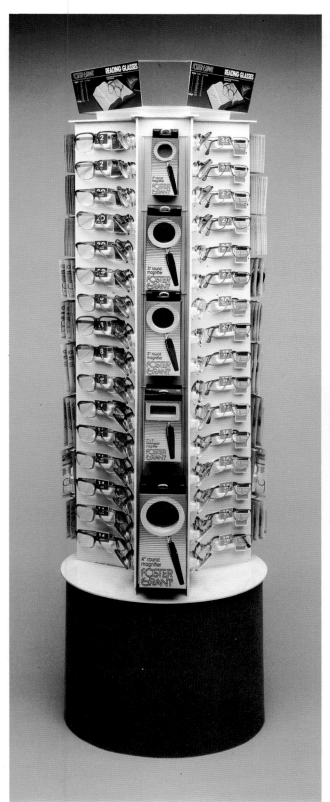

Advertiser: Foster Grant
Producer: Flair Industries, Providence, RI
Designers: Bob Shelton and Norman Saucier

This rotating display holds 96 pairs of reading glasses in its three main panels. The narrow insert areas hold magnifying glasses and carded eyewear accessories like nose pads, hinge rings, chains and straps, and so on. The insert wires are removable for cleaning and to adjust to a change of product.

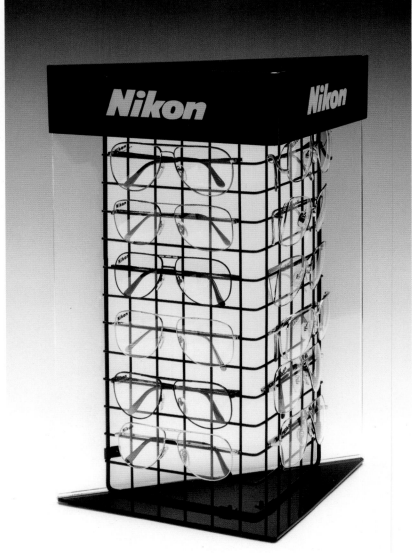

Advertiser: Sterling Optical Corp.
Producer: Brinker Displays, E. Orange, NJ

Bold colors and sharp lines give this display a clean, hi-tech look. Whether hung on a wall or placed on a counter, it fits its environment.

Advertiser: Ektelon
Producer: Trenmark, La Mirada, CA

Glasses designed especially for racquetball players can easily be examined when they are displayed in this countertop unit. Extra stock can be kept on the other sides of the display.

Advertiser: McNeil Sunglass Co.
Producer: Process Displays Inc.,
New Berlin, WI

This counter display, with its built-in mirror, tempts the customer to try on a pair of these fashion sunglasses. The unit, which has glasses on both sides, was vacuum formed, stained and wiped, and then assembled by hand.

Advertiser: Titleist (via Packaging Consultants Inc.)
Producer: Associated Packaging Inc., West Deptford, NJ

This successful display can be used as a floor or a counter stand.

Advertiser: Wilson Sporting Goods Co.
Producer: Visual Marketing Inc., Chicago
Designer: Larry Zock

This floor stand is designed to help golfers choose for themselves the golf club that most closely meets their individual needs. Each of the four faces demonstrates, with sample clubs, one of the four critical areas of consideration. The customer can try out a club for length, lie angle, shaft flex, and grip size, using actual clubs, and decide which is right for him. He can then write out his personal specifications on an order blank.

Advertiser: Wilson Sporting Goods Co.
Producer: RTC Industries, Inc., Chicago

An unusual ball-shaped header and a colorful base call attention to this display, designed for pro shops and sports stores. It holds as many as 96 cans, and fits into the tightest corner.

Advertiser: Best Products Co., Inc.
Producer: Marketing Displays Inc.,
Farmington Hills, MI

This self-standing unit implements a compact and complete ''self-merchandising'' operation. Laminated catalog sheets are displayed in a tamper-proof ring binding, permanently mounted to the table. Pockets hold supplies of pencils and order forms. The system occupies only about 3 square feet in the store, and saves the expense of one person in the store.

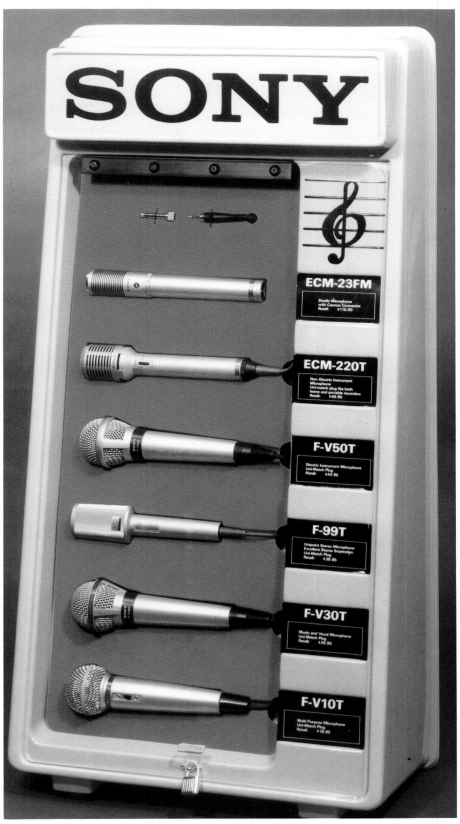

Advertiser: Sony
Producer: Displayco East, Newark, NJ
Designer: Jamie Bauer

Each product stands out against a red flocked vacuum formed tray enclosed in a styrene shell and protected by a clear plexiglass door.

Advertiser: Hanes Underalls
Producer: Thomas A. Schutz Co., Inc., Morton Grove, IL
Designer: Edmond A. Giroux

The unusual angling of the product in this floor display gave the product greater visibility as the consumer came down the aisle, as well as permitting more product facings in the limited space.

Advertiser: Mont Blanc/Koh-i-Noor
Producer: Palmer Display Associates Inc.,
Kenilworth, NJ

This elegant counter display adds glamor to these top-of-the-line writing instruments. The locked case, with its built-in light and mirrored back wall, allows the consumer to see all sides of the pens. There is a drawer in the base of the unit which can be used for writing accessories or for literature.

Advertiser: Pakula Fashion Jewelry
Producer: Astra Products Inc., Paterson, NJ
Designer: Thomas Mulvihill

The modular nature of this system allows a wide variety of counter, wall, or floor displays. Slatwall adapters accommodate any suitable product or product holder.

Advertiser: Generic
Producer: Astra Products Inc., Paterson, NJ
Designer: Tom Strasser

Injection-molded components can be put together in various sizes and capacities at a relatively modest cost. Adapters are available for necklaces, chains, and bracelets, as well as for mirrors.

Advertiser: Kirie Fine Jewelry
Producer: Astra Products Inc., Paterson, NJ

By offsetting these two display chests, eye-catching mirrors can be placed in the corners to add to the attractiveness of the pilfer-proof display of small jewelry boxes.

Advertiser: Elizabeth Morrey Inc.
Producer: Astra Products Inc., Paterson, NJ
Designer: Carol

The demand was for a high-capacity jewelry display for supermarkets that kept the items out of the reach of toddlers. Here clear hooks glued directly to the unit held 3 cards, allowing the unit a maximum capacity of 972 cards.

Advertiser: Monet Jewelers
Producer: Trans World Marketing, East Rutherford, NJ

Triangular towers, sleek in black and gold, can be used in single, double, or triple configurations. Each triangular face can be devoted to a single style or color, thus, segregating the faces for different theme and color stories. For those stores which desired it, the individual pieces could be locked in, so the consumer could touch, but not remove, an individual piece of jewelry.

Advertiser: Konica USA Inc.
Producer: Trans World Marketing, East Rutherford, NJ

This unit merchandises three cameras in very limited display space (less than 6 square inches on the counter). The back of the display has selling information to aid the retailer to talk about these cameras.

Advertiser: Konica USA Inc.
Producer: Trans World Marketing, East Rutherford, NJ

Placed on the cash register, the side that faces the customer reinforces the brand name and image, while the rear carries a tax table for the convenience of the store person using the register. Made of vacuum formed plastic with hot stamping, the full color elements are tipped-on lithography.

Advertiser: Bantam Books
Producer: Deijon Inc., Carlstadt, NJ
Designer: Vince Gambello

Designed to merchandise Bantam's Sweet Dreams line, the purple masonite panels, silkscreened with the line's logo, emphasizes the romance genre of the product.

Advertiser: B. Dalton Booksellers
Producer: Deijon Inc., Carlstadt, NJ
Designer: Wolf Dietrich Hannecke

A freestanding, rotating display has spring-loaded racks which keep magazines in place and displayed in an orderly fashion.

Advertiser: SRS
Producer: Boise Cascade Corp.,
Sunnyvale, CA
Designer: Robert Marlin

This counter display holds books in the upper level, while the drawer below gives access to corresponding audio cassettes.

Advertiser: Sears, Roebuck & Co.
Producer: Rapid Mounting and Finishing Co., Chicago

This display, or rather group of display elements, was intend to tie in with retail advertising and to promote a two-department line of branded clothing. The elements could be mounted to foam core, chipboard and masonite, on the wall, on end caps, and suspended from the ceiling.

Advertiser: Waldenbooks
Producer: The Synn-Comm Group Inc., New York
Designer: Kenneth Curtis

This mobile self-contained unit is designed to be rolled out to the entrance of the store and easily returned to the store space after closing. Coming in three widths, as well as in a version with product on both sides, the shelves can hold audio or video tapes as well as books.

Advertiser: The New Yorker Magazine
Producer: The Synn-Comm Group Inc., New York
Designer: Kenneth Curtis

This display was thermo-formed in three-dimensional metallic plastic, to recreate the feeling of the New York skyline.

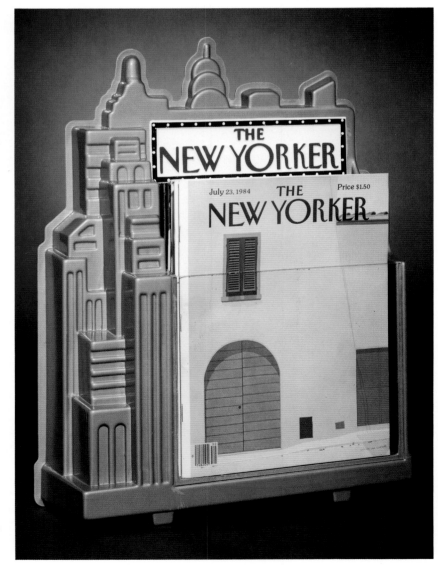

Advertiser: Generic
Producer: Deijon Inc., Carlstadt, NJ

This heavy-duty, front-end merchandiser offers impulse items at the check-out counter, but when the lane is closed, the end section swings around to block access, and utilizes the blocked space for more product display.

Advertiser: Artcarved Class Rings
Producer: Brinker Displays, E. Orange, NJ

To thwart pilfering of small, but valuable items, the side door on the outer acrylic case can be locked, and the unit comes with a wire cable to secure it to the counter.

Advertiser: L.A. Gear
Producer: United California Display, South Gate, CA
Designers: Clover Howard and Jim Ong

The life-size figure and background was designed to create high visibility for the fashion athletic footwear during the busy back-to-school shopping season.

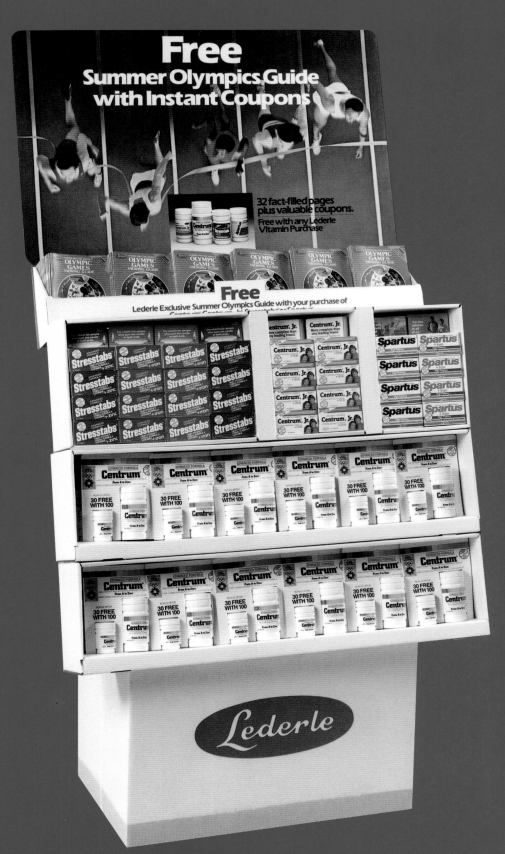

Advertiser: Lederle Laboratories
Producer: Henschel-Steinau, Inc.,
                   Englewood, NJ

Holding 144 packages of assorted product, the logistics were simplified by using three separate corrugatesd shelves. The display was easy to set up, showed the products and the near-pack premium, as well as a sweepstakes.

Advertiser: Scholl Inc.
Producer: Henschel-Steinau, Inc., Englewood, NJ

Injection-molded legs on the bottom tray raise the display 4'' off the ground for ease of mopping. Snap together construction allows set-up in a few minutes without the use of tools. Each tray has a fold-up divider which angles the product upward and places two graphic panels within the side supports.

Advertiser: Levi Jeans
Producer: Color 2000 Inc., San Francisco

The large hanging frame permits the display of a large photo print without mounting, which simplifies handling since it permits the print to be rolled up for shipping.

Advertiser: Durban Inc. (Intermezzo)
Producer: Popco Display Inc., Tokyo
Designers: Takayoshi Teraki and
Michiko Yoshida

This family of signing uses block letters, sometimes three-dimensional of logo brick, to gain continuity, which is helped by the use of dark gray and permanent yellow.

POINT OF PURCHASE—Rx FOR INCREASED PROFITS

ROBERT A. HOGSETT
Director of Promotional Services
Consumer Products Div., A.H. Robins Co.
RICHMOND, VA

There are spiraling changes in point-of-purchase advertising which are linked to technological influences evident in the graphics world of today. With each new electronic, scientific or communicating technique comes newer discoveries in point-of-purchase know-how.

From caveman's graffiti, to barber poles and wooden Indians all the way to the science fiction of tomorrow, we are constantly paving the way to newer, futuristic point-of-purchase materials for advertising our wares. Even though the struggle is needless, it is novel, exciting, and establishes a craving for selling at all levels in business today. This selling activity produced a record purchase of over $13 billion in point-of-purchase materials in 1988 and is projected to escalate dramatically in succeeding years.

Looking at what we use for point-of-purchase today is like looking at yesterday's newspaper. The implications are newsworthy, informative, but out-of-date, and merely establish stepping stones for tomorrow's planning. To stay ahead of the spiral, we must continue to think to the future in increments of two to five years, depending on the type of planning, acting, or production involved. As we become even more professional, point-of-purchase becomes more than a cost of doing business. Produced properly and opportunely, it becomes an investment that adds profit, prestige, and that all-important contributor to the selling efforts.

Point-of-purchase has the potential of being an "Rx" for "growing profits" a means for overcoming competitive price-wars and other complications in a wheeler/dealer environment. Point-of-purchase can best segmentize the marketplace, being specific to needs, uses, and can direct the message to the prospect who is in the buying mode.

With the trendsetting information crisis upon us, we as customers are beginning to want, need, and even use too much, too quickly for available shelf space. P-O-P gives retailers the flexibility of coping with volatile marketing and selling activities.

This then begins a new era of coping with more changing and spiraling circumstances, requiring retailers and marketers to make more P-O-P available to maintain flexibility while altering tactical planning and execution to meet the varying uncontrolled influences on the markets.

Between now and the 1990s, we can expect changes in a number of ways:

■ A reduction and change in couponing methods...The increased concern for counterfeiting, the clutter in many markets, and increasing redemption expenses will reduce couponing in today's manner and will force shifts to more innovative electronic methods.

■ Materials will improve and be better controlled...Engineering, production and distribution will all be affected. We can expect improved methods for carrying the message to the customer. Along with this will come a new awareness of the value of point-of-purchase materials and an improved usage ratio.

■ We can expect an increased concern and need for health care products along with the P-O-P promotional tools...With newer and deeper concern for health and appearance in an aging society, more point-of-purchase will be engineered as attention-getting devices for drawing dramatic attention to the product to influence the purchase.

■ Retailers will be looking for readily available, prepacked promotions...With major takeovers producing larger retailing influences, added to increased pressure toward cutting costs, we can expect more efforts to be given to centralized distribution. This will bring pressure on manufacturers to combine their packaging techniques, so as to provide a complete packaged promotional unit that is in tune with a seasonal or specific promotional emphasis. Retailers will devote more time and effort in support of combined purchasing and promotional efforts. This means that manufacturers must be able to provide merchandise in combination with display and all promotional support material as a unit for retail distribution on a timely basis.

■ Point-of-purchase will play a newer public service role and help to improve communications between the manufacturer and the retailer...Along with concern for liability, customer acceptance and misrepresentation of product, retailers and manufacturers will be in communication in a new supportive role to prevent overdosages, excessive usage, or to protect ineffectiveness of products based on the lack of understanding as to indications. Manufacturers will continue to be protective of their products and become more active in protecting customers, the retailers, and themselves by supplying specific P-O-P materials in an effort to be more informative.

■ Spiraling electronic developments will play a major role in point-of-purchase advertising...We can expect the use of closed circuit and cable television to develop means and methods for customers to interact—to read ECGs, renew prescriptions, determine the need for vitamins, the level of cholesterol, heart disease symptoms, pregnancy testing, as well as other problems and all such symptomatic conditions dealing with health, drugs, and toiletry products. All this is expected to generate more need for P-O-P sales support materials which will be designed to stimulate the customer's interest in, need of, and loyalty to specific products.

As more women work outside of the home, they will be spending less time shopping and are less concerned about costs. This will lead to more and greater attention-getting display materials which will attract the customer to particular brands, needs, advantages, and price savings benefits. It will also tend to increase the amount of impulse purchasing.

Point-of-purchase materials can contribute as much to gross sales as the advertising media, but working together, campaigns can yield sales increases of 500 percent to 700 percent! According to POPAI/DuPont studies, many of the health care product categories are impulse purchases, with 50 and more percent of shoppers making their brand selections during their visits to the store, and thus, greatly subject to point-of-purchase influence.

For all these reasons, we can expect that point-of-purchase will play an ever increasing role in marketing in this field, and will be recognized at the "Rx" for increased profits in the drug and general toiletries markets of the 1990s.

Advertiser: Kurlash/Diamon Deb Ltd.
Producer: David Brace Displays Inc.,
Lancaster, NY

A two-sided space saver uses only 1½ square feet of valuable marketing space. Vacuum-formed plastic, special hooks and track, and varied product layout combine to make this an effective merchandiser.

Advertiser: Lever Brothers
Producer: Henschel-Steinau, Inc.,
Englewood, NJ

This two-sided floor merchandiser will hold 14 dozen Pepsodent toothbrushes with room for competitive brands. With only four pieces, including the vacuum-formed product trays, it is easy to set up.

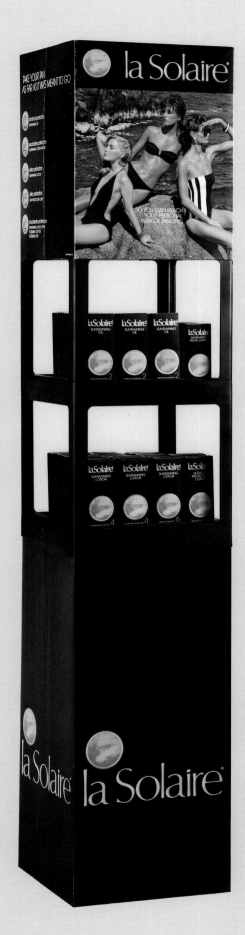

Advertiser: Plough, Inc.
Producer: Henschel-Steinau, Inc.,
Englewood, NJ

The colors of the beautiful
packaging were continued by the
black trays and supports, both
injection-molded, and the bold four
color process lithgraphy which was
laminated to all four sides of both
the sign and the base.

Advertiser: Smith Kline Consumer Products
Producer: Decorr, Div. of Hughes
                Containers Ltd., Toronto

This corrugated merchandiser was
designed to get off-shelf placement
for a seasonal product.

Advertiser: Scott Paper Co.
Producer: The Acorn Group, Chicago
Designer: James Lauro

These display racks, of injection-molded plastic, shipped flat to reduce freight expense, but were easy to set up and install in existing toilet tissue shelf sections. The package was clearly visible to provide reinforcement of the product as shown on television.

Advertiser: Barnes Hind Inc.
Producer: Patrick H. Joyce and Associates, Des Plaines, IL

This unit was designed to help a doctor select the proper fit of prepackaged soft contact lenses while working with a patient. The smoked acrylic rack holds four trays, each with 50 vials arranged by magnification and other correction needs.

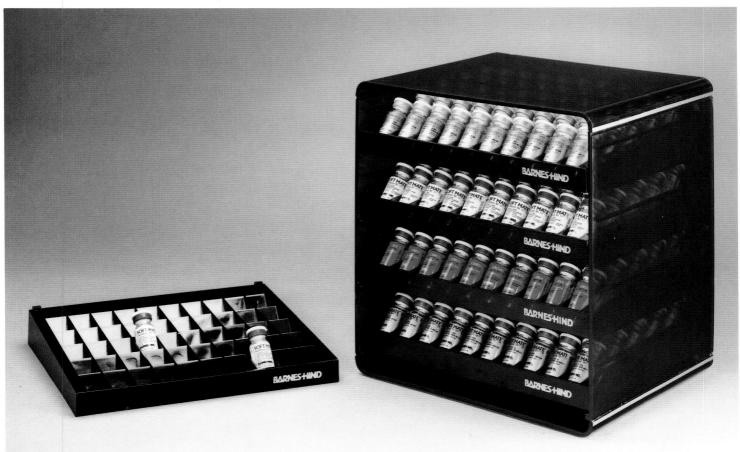

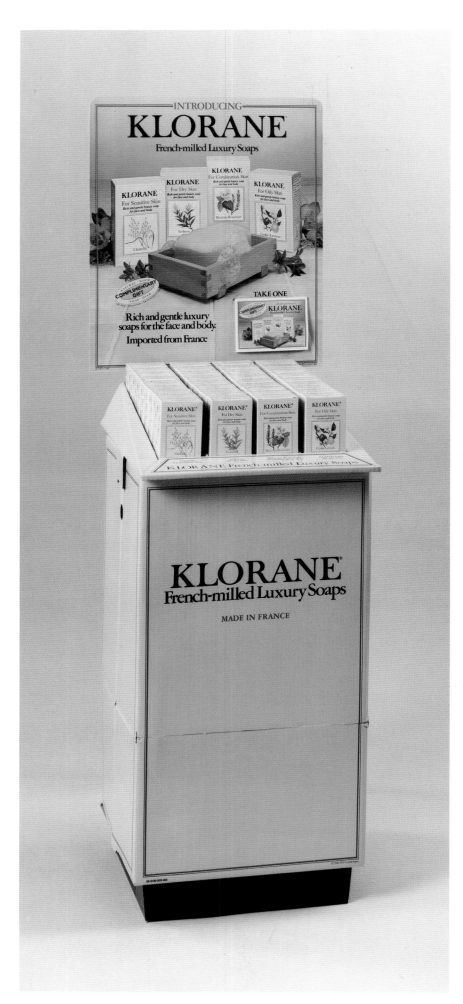

Advertiser: Clairol, Inc.
Producer: Henschel-Steinau, Inc.,
Englewood, NJ

Through the use of a preprinted liner, a compact corrugated floor display with bold graphics attractively displays 36 pieces of expensive Klorane soap. The unit is shipped prepacked and easily assembles in a few minutes.

Advertiser: Mennen Canada
Producer: Innovators Inc., Toronto

This dump bin display was supplemented by an overhead mobile featuring the same baseball diamond used on the header. This promoted a consumer contest, and the promotion was backed up by a dealer contest.

Advertiser: 3M
Producer: RTC Industries, Inc., Chicago

This display, which has four 15 sq. ft. shelves, can handle any combination of BufPuf products in volumes nine to ten times higher than can be handled in ordinary shelving. The clear, flared-out dump bin on the bottom shelf creates a bargain environment for whichever product is placed there.

MEETING VARIED NEEDS

JOSEPH PALAMARA
Director, Display Development
Coty
NEW YORK, NY

The requirements for P-O-P advertising in the cosmetic and fragrance category vary considerably from those in other display categories. Many of the products are not basic necessities; the display must not only attract the consumer, but convince him/her of a "need" for the product. The emphasis in merchandising this type of product is, and must continue to be, on what it will do for the consumer—make you beautiful, make you sensual, make you healthier—and therefore make you want to have it. A display may carry a wide range of makeup, colors, and fragrances, along with testers or shade charts, to allow a consumer to establish the look or image of their choice. All this must be done within a limited area, with a limited amount of copy, with a very limited amount of selling time, and with a design that is appropriate to the assigned outlet.

These outlets range from elegant department stores to mass drug chains to supermarkets, each requiring its own form of P-O-P to satisfy its own image. For the higher priced lines in the better department stores, the use of materials like corian, glass, plastic and even marble have created an elegant, quality look that is desired by both the merchandisers and the outlet. For the mass outlets, where more product must be merchandised for a shorter period of time and at a lower cost, the design of P-O-P becomes more difficult. However, clever use of less expensive materials can be extremely effective. Vacuum-formed displays with a limited use of injection-molded parts, and the use of vacuum-formed risers with printed material give dimension, with a look of permanence.

There has been an increasing trend to coordinate displays with national advertising—TV and magazine ads—to maintain a desired product image. By repeating in the display the key points created in other forms of advertising, the consumer is alerted to the product at the most crucial time—the time of decision. With marketing, advertising, and P-O-P working together at an early stage, a more effective overall selling program can be achieved.

Computer technology is the current trend in many businesses. It is natural that this has been introduced into P-O-P, and interactive displays are being developed for many product categories. This will, indeed, be appropriate for some of them, but how well this will work in the area of cosmetics and fragrances will take some time to determine. There may not be a substitute for the live feel and smell of a product, as well as the actual test of it on *your* skin. The interactive display can be a guide to color combinations but the final decision is made with live product. Additionally, in an industry that moves so quickly with fashion trends, is highly promotional, and where displays in the mass market are up for a limited time, interactive displays may not be appropriate.

Designers in the cosmetic area will continue to develop and combine different kinds of materials with attractive illustrations and product testers, but the most dramatic change in the future will be in the form the testers take. Due to the hazards of consumers' sharing live cosmetic testers in stores, there are laws being considered (and enacted) that will require individual samples at the point of sale. This is being developed in the industry in different ways, to satisfy the following criteria: one, to give the consumer a sample of product to test that has not been exposed to anyone else; two, to give the consumer a sample for color (or fragrance); and three, to give the consumer something to take away. The form these new testers take will be a challenge to the designers and will affect the design of P-O-P material.

The cosmetic and fragrance category of P-O-P has been one of the leaders of innovative displays, and its designers will continue to explore new and different materials and designs. It is not as blue sky an industry with unlimited resources as it may seem to be. Designers of P-O-P for cosmetic and fragrance products have distinct goals and cost limitations. What they have done attests to the success they have had in filling these needs. The future promises to be even more challenging and exciting for any involved in this industry.

Advertiser: Christian Dior
Producer: Consumer Promotions Inc.,
Mt. Vernon, NY

This injection-molded unit places the testable products within easy reach of the consumer. The clear acrylic dome showcases the products not designed for testing.

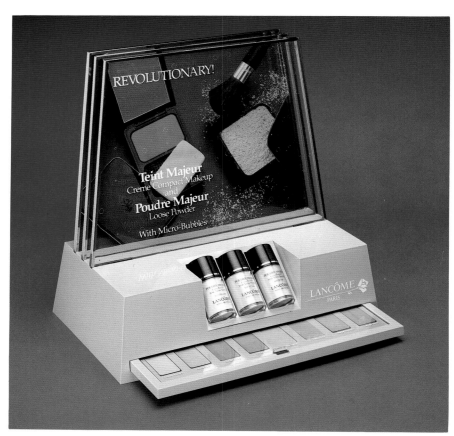

Advertiser: Lancome
Producer: Brinker Displays,
East Orange, NJ

To permit consumers to test these new products themselves, the tester pans are easily available by pulling open the door. A clear cover protects the pans.

Advertiser: Christian Dior Perfumes Inc.
Producer: Displayco East Inc., Newark, NJ
Designer: Joyce Galello

The plexiglass header is attached to the base after shipping, thus simplifying packing and reducing shipping damage. All products are easily accessible and testable, with all shades being shown and identified.

Advertiser: Coty Inc.
Producer: Trans World Marketing, East Rutherford, NJ

The sky blue styrene base merchandiser complements product packaging. Its simulated woven edge helps to portray the desired seasonal theme and its feminine feeling. A dominant live tester encourages trial and purchase.

Advertiser: Noxell
Producer: Thomson-Leeds Co. Inc., New York

An elegant vacuum-formed base and riser was created to complement the four-color lithographed riser.

Advertiser: Lancome
Producer: Brinker Displays,
East Orange, NJ

This display introduces two new products. It holds no live product or tester, but is a three-dimensional graphic panel to enlighten consumers about the new products.

Advertiser: Colonia
Producer: Consumer Promotions Inc.,
Mt. Vernon, NY

This small display launched a new men's product, while having a halo effect by reminding the consumer of the companion woman's fragrance.The bottle's concept highlights the entire theme of the

attractive cherry wood base, tie into the distinctive bottle design. The larger bottle tilts easily and safely for product sampling.

Advertiser: Geoffrey Beene
Producer: Ledan Inc., New York

The unique packaging material was picked up in the display backgrounds, while a natural linen look was used in the vacuum formed bases. The picture on the larger display tied in with the introductory ads.

Advertiser: Coty Inc.
Producer: Trans World Marketing,
East Rutherford, NJ.

This program consisted of two vacuum formed merchandisers with live tester areas, a styrene department store tester, and other ancillary point-of-purchase materials. The program makes a strong visual statement, reinforcing the image by using metallic colorized plastic with the subtle radiuses of bottle and logo.

Advertiser: Coty Inc.
Producer: Trans World Marketing,
East Rutherford, NJ

This colorful display was designed to merchandise gift sets. Its four shelves allow for a mixed variety of products. It took 25 percent less space than the previous year's display, while increasing the product load by 25 percent.

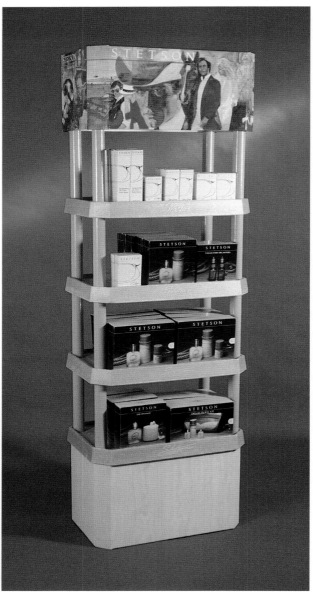

Advertiser: Sanofi Beauty Products
Producer: Consumer Promotions Inc.,
Mt. Vernon, NY

This dramming unit picks up the gold metal and tortoise shell of the packages and bottles to help build the image of luxury.

Advertiser: Parfums Ungaro
Producer: Consumer Promotions Inc.,
Mt. Vernon, NY

This dramming unit incorporates the round, soft curves suggested by the package, with gold and silver metals adding to the elegance of the display.

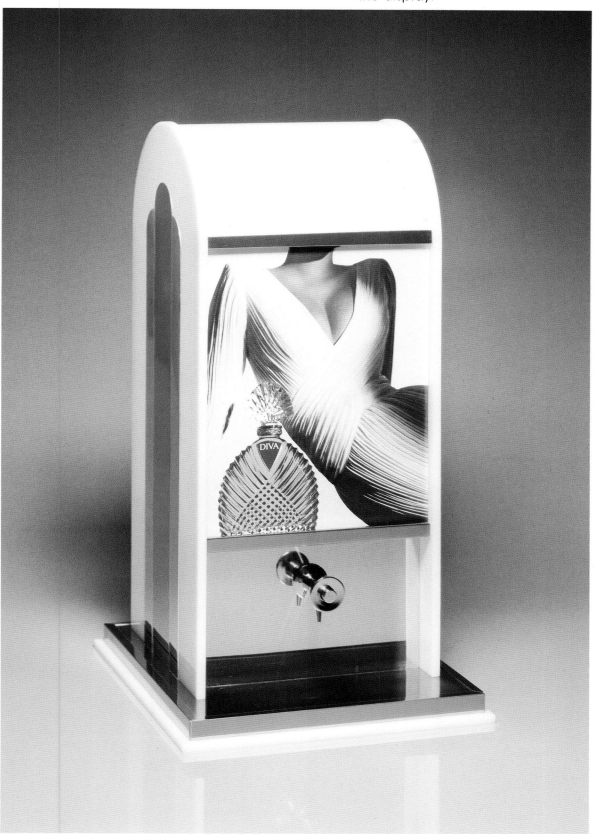

Advertiser: Jovan/Beecham
Producer: Patrick H. Joyce and Associates,
Des Plaines, IL

This family of displays obtained
space for the new male fragrance
line in various retail locations.

Advertiser: Elizabeth Arden
Producer: Trans World Marketing,
East Rutherford, NJ

A stage setting of quality materials
and simple elegant soft curves
complement the bottle design and
act as a frame, drawing attention
to the graphic insert and bottle. The
four-color lithographic can be
easily changed.

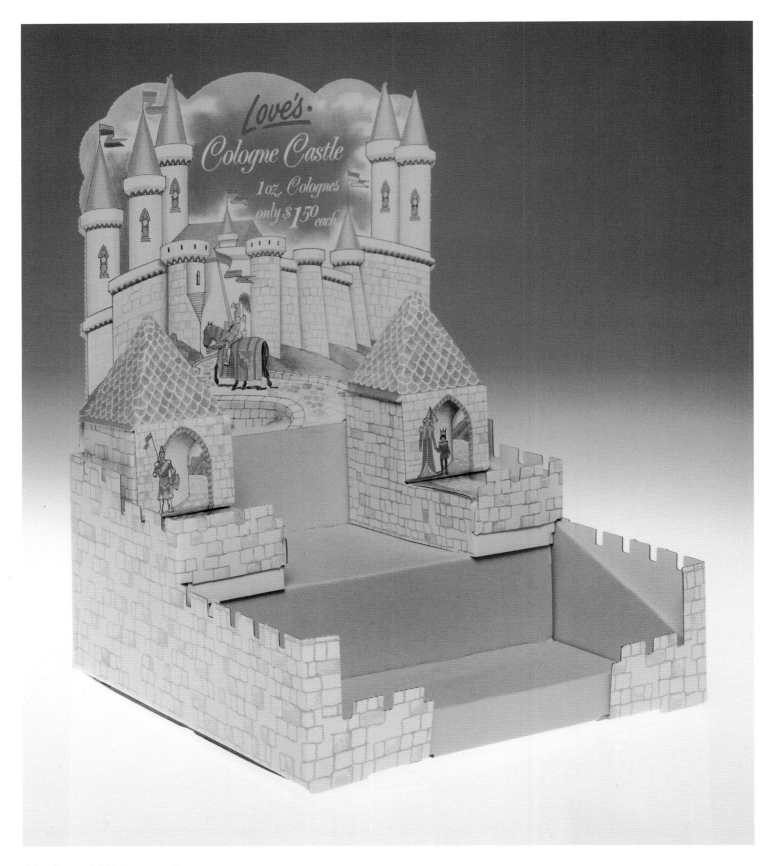

Advertiser: MEM Company Inc.
Producer: Associated Packaging Inc.,
West Deptford, NJ
Designer: William Manteufel

This counter unit was used for the
trial size of this new cologne, and
carried through the castle theme.

Advertiser: Maybelline USA
Producer: Trans World Marketing,
East Rutherford, NJ

The safari theme is developed in the base and riser to highlight unusual nail colors inspired by African fashions. The nail chip tester bar is integrated into the base, and encourages impulse purchases. The chipboard bottom allowed the unit to be attached to the company's stock floor stand in accounts without counter space.

Advertiser: Jacquelin Cochran
Producer: Consumer Promotions Inc.,
Mt. Vernon, NY

This unit, which dispenses samples of the product, were designed to be set up on tables during lunches sponsored by Maxim's, and to reflect the Maxim name and logo.

Advertiser: Chanel No. 5
Producer: Thomson-Leeds Co. Inc.,
New York

This counter display maintains Chanel's classic look with fabricated pure white plastic and gold graphics. The three-tier presentation of product gives a contemporary look and shows a good line of product in a limited space.

Advertiser: Coty Inc.
Producer: Trans World Marketing, East Rutherford, NJ

These three counter displays are part of a major program to introduce the idea that there is a relationship between the mood of a fragrance and the colors of cosmetics. Four separate fragrances were used in this promotion, and each has its own display unit, with the mood indicated by the model shown. The vacuum formed trays were made from the same basic mold, with modular tooling to handle variations in the fragrance packaging.

Advertiser: Noxell
Producer: The Howard Marlboro Group, New York

The unit fits into the product display, suspended on pegboard in a free-standing rack, or perched at the end of an in-line unit. The customer answers the questions posed by the computer screen by touching keys on a membrane keyboard. The screen then makes it recommendations, and women can pick up the specified products from the display. The computer is small, battery-powered, and easy to replace as a unit.

Advertiser: Clairol Inc.
Producer: Henschel-Steinau, Inc., Englewood, NJ

In an effort to encourage the sampling of the product, the manufacturer distributed a fixture of clear plastic which incorporated a metal clamp. A bottle with a pump top replacing the normal screw top could be placed in front of the shelf display, and the fixture was sturdy enough to permit the consumer to test the lotion.

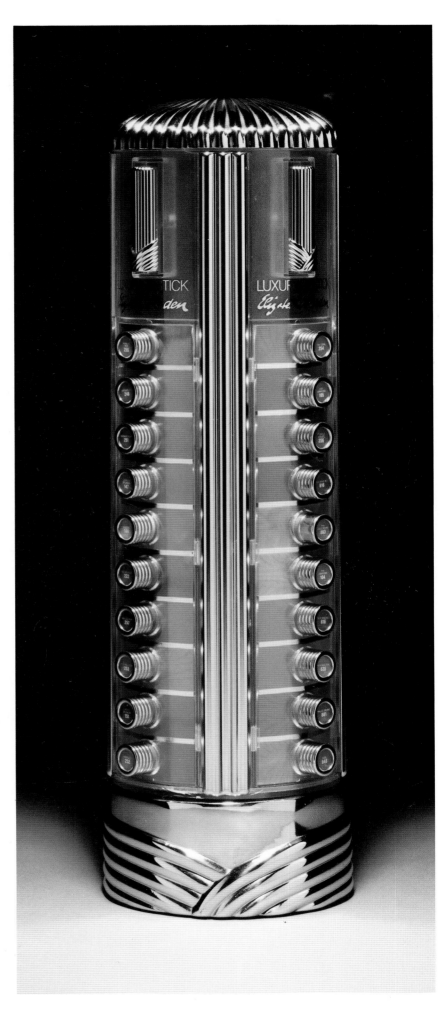

Advertiser: Elizabeth Arden
Producer: Consumer Promotions Inc.,
Mt. Vernon, NY

This luxurious unit, which borrows the design elements of the product on display, demonstrates a complete line of color samples. The color inserts can be changed, allowing flexibility as seasons and fashions change.

Advertiser: The Gillette Co.
Producer: Creative Displays Inc., Chicago

This floor merchandiser holds not only stock, take-home samples, and a touch tester, but also a battery-operated computer that helps the consumer select the appropriate products. The base offers storage space for overstocked products. A variation is designed for use on counters.

Advertiser: Dermablend Corrective Cosmetics

Producer: Brinker Displays, East Orange, NJ

Designed to incorporate three displays into one, this unit houses Dermablend's full line of corrective cosmetics. The leg cover tubes are held in a vertical position for immediate product identification.

Advertiser: Maybelline USA
Producer: Trans World Marketing,
East Rutherford, NJ

The domed package shape was
carried over into the design of this
counter display, and permitted 12
product facings in a clean,
compact unit. Live product testers
helped move the product.

Advertiser: Pantene
Producer: The Howard Marlboro Group,
New York

When not in use, the screen on this island display continuously shows animated graphics designed to stop the customer. When she touches the screen as requested, she is automatically guided through a series of questions. She selects her responses by touching the screen, and this determines which products she should use, and then issues a print-out of Pantene's beauty prescriptions. She can then make her selection from the stock on the lower shelves.

Advertiser: S.C. Johnson & Son Inc.
Producer: Creative Displays Inc., Chicago

Used to introduce a new product line, this unit ships as a compact prepack. The product is packed in trays that interlock to increase product visibility, while dividers provide easy product access.

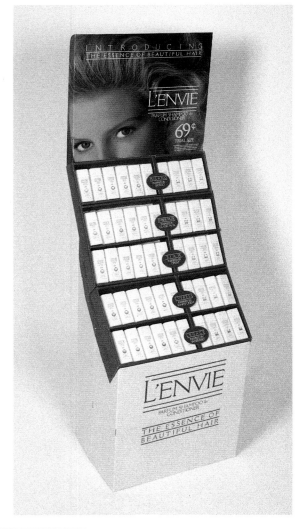

Advertiser: L'Oreal
Producer: Consumer Promotions Inc., Mt. Vernon, NY

This display, which contains one each of all the products in the Plenitude line, gives the customer the opportunity of testing any of them. A pamphlet describing the product benefits is centrally located.

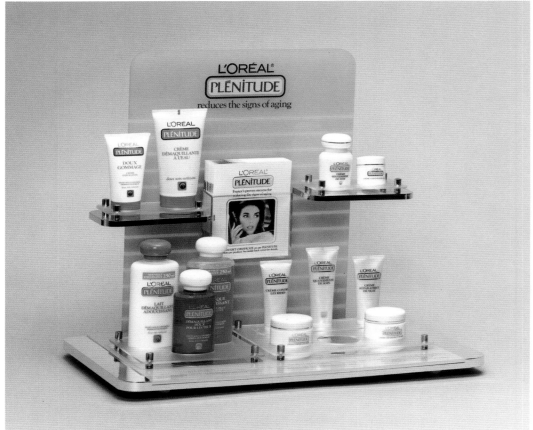

Advertiser: The Gillette Company
Producer: Displayco East Inc., Newark, NJ

This prepacked floor stand is easy to assemble. The vacuum formed tray, with its staggered compartments, attracts the eye, and presents the four scents that are available. The graphics picks up the theme from print and television advertising.

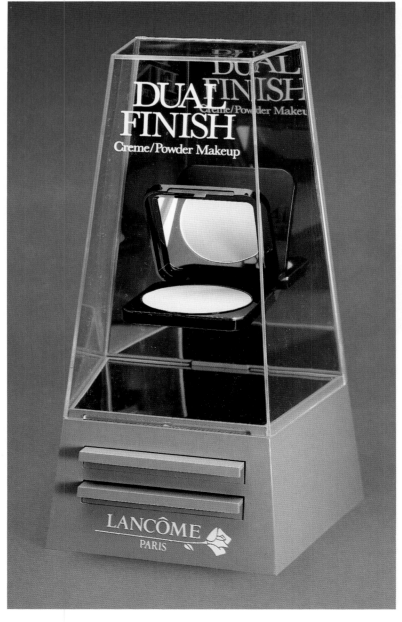

Advertiser: Lancome
Producer: Brinker Displays, East Orange, NJ

This display announces a change in packaging to a more up-scale presentation with its "Jewel Box" design. The compact design allows the unit to stay on the counter longer.

Advertiser: Chesebrough-Pond's (Canada) Inc.
Producer: Decorr, Div. of Hughes Containers Ltd., Toronto

This corrugated floor stand holds both shampoo and conditioner, each in its own distinctive way.

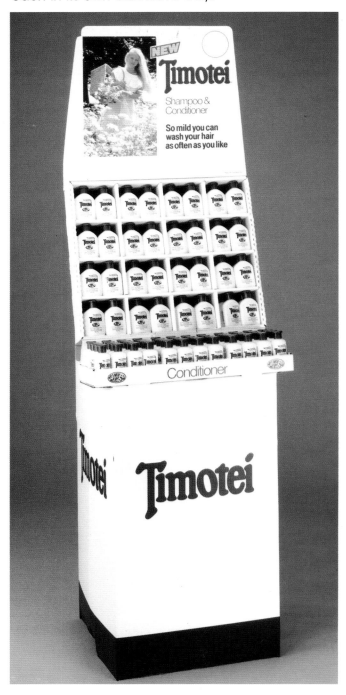

Advertiser: Soft Sheen Products
Producer: Creative Displays Inc., Chicago

Shipped as a prepack, the slim base lifts the back half tray to give the customer easier access to the back rows of the product.

Advertiser: Christian Dior
Producer: Consumer Promotions Inc.,
Mt. Vernon, NY

This major display shows the entire
product line at one time, and has
provisions for test samples. The
storage drawers, accessible from
the rear, holds products to be sold
by store personnel.

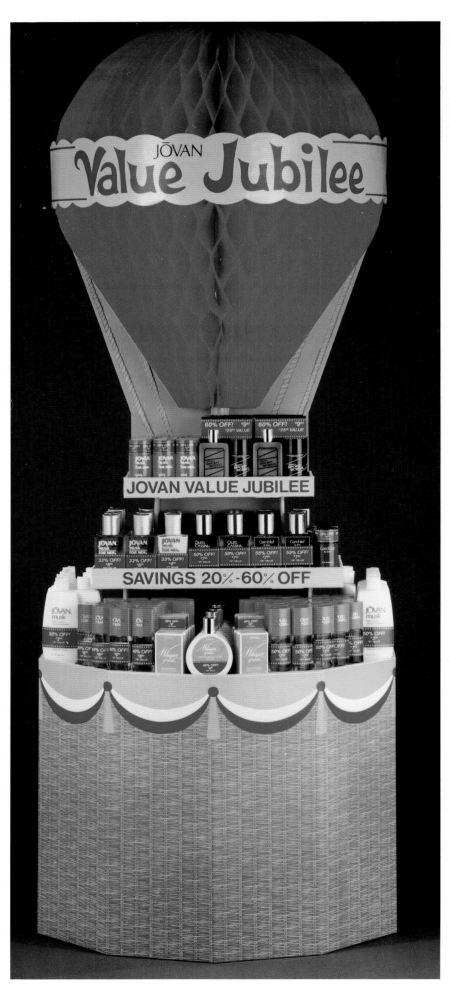

Advertiser: Jovan/Beecham
Producer: Patrick H. Joyce and Associates, Des Plaines, IL

The honeycomb paper balloon and the base, printed with a basket weave, attracted attention to a special post-Christmas sale.

Advertiser: Redken Laboratories
Producer: United California Display, South Gate, CA

Intended for use in Beauty salons, this unit on wheels gives flexibility in display, with auxiliary units that can be attached. It is easily assembled with a single tool.

Advertiser: Beecham (Canada) Inc.
Producer: Decorr, Div. of Hughes
Containers Ltd., Toronto

This counter display is made of corrugated board, lithographed in four colors, and produced at half the cost of a conventional styrene tray.

Advertiser: Clairol
Producer: Displayco East Inc., Newark, NJ
Designer: Gene Giacumbo

The bright red base and the unusual diagonal structure calls attention to this prepacked floor display used as part of an introductory campaign. The use of silver mylar and colorcast paper added to its appeal.

Advertiser: Noxell
Producer: Consumer Promotions Inc.,
Mt. Vernon, NY

This compact counter-top unit holds
stock for four color groups in a
seasonal promotion.

Advertiser: L'Oreal
Producer: Consumer Promotions Inc., Mt. Vernon, NY

This unit, which can stand on the counter or be hung on a pegwall background, is a unique way of educating consumers regarding eye make-up coordination. The leaves can easily be flipped open to any page, where springs hold them open. The lithographed inserts are easily changed for updating.

ADIEU TO RECREATIONAL SHOPPING

LOU SZEPI
Director Environment Design Services
Hallmark Cards Incorporated
KANSAS CITY, MO

The marketplace has changed dramatically in recent years. The enormous influence of recreational shopping has waned dramatically; more women work now than those that stay at home raising their families. The growth of the regional mall has slowed while the mass merchandising chains have grown dramatically.

Personal communications, either by the spoken word or the written word, continue to occupy an important place in our lengthening list of social obligations—social obligations that must be fulfilled by consumers with time deficits and who are basically time-poor in their ability to fulfill family and social obligations. To this picture add various lifestyles emerging among consumers; each lifestyle with its own unique wants and needs for personal communications, and what we find is a rather confusing and complicated point-of-purchase picture emerging.

The present trend emerging in merchandising of greeting cards, gift wrap and party goods is that it is no longer possible to attempt to be all things to all people, but rather to attempt to identify and target consumer segments and then cater to them by providing a focused merchandising statement to attract these targeted consumers.

Consumers, once identified, must be treated to a shopping experience that makes a clear quality statement to them in a contracted period of time. The consumer must understand clearly and quickly what it is that he or she is looking at, the first time it is seen. The shopping experience must make the most out of their limited time, while still providing them a pleasurable shopping experience.

In addition, the merchandising must be esthetically pleasing, focused on the targeted consumer segments, and provide a visual information message as to the product's end use. It must also make an overall statement of quality, thus allowing the consumer to make an educated buying decision in a timely manner.

In today's marketplace, point-of-purchase merchandising of stationery products plays a key role for the retailer by allowing the right product to be placed in the right place at the right time.

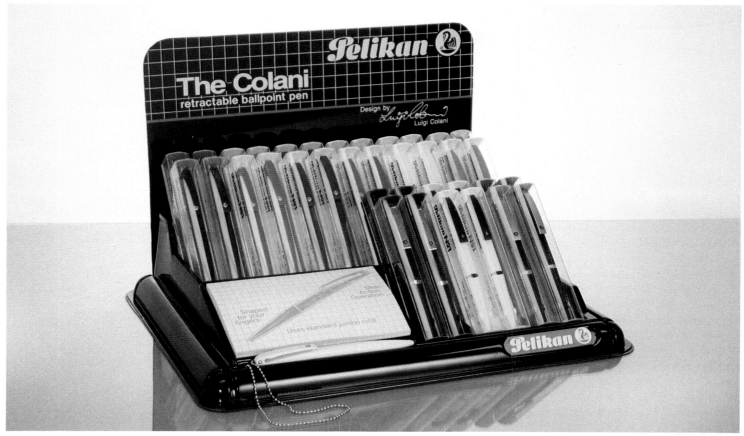

Advertiser: Pelikan Pen
Producer: Trans World Marketing,
East Rutherford, NJ

This new pen was shaped to fit the hand, so it was important to get purchasers to try it out. A counter display held an assortment of pens in an easy-to-grasp position, and a pad of paper right in front, so people were tempted to pick it up and use it.

Advertiser: Faber Castell Corp.
Producer: Trans World Marketing,
East Rutherford, NJ

With four brands within the line of metal roller point pens, a tall and narrow display was created for each brand. The small footprint of the displays allowed for placement in key register locations, but the units snap together whenever space is available. Headers of various sizes are furnished for different installations.

Advertiser: Gibson Greeting Card Co.
Producer: AMD Industries Inc., Chicago
Designer: Sharon Young

Each of the trays on this twin rotating merchandiser has a removable divider to permit inclusion of jumbo cards in the display. The caption strip channels can be easily replaced, and there are reorder ticket channels for each pocket.

Advertiser: Light Impressions
Producer: Boise Cascade Corp.,
Sunnyvale, CA
Designer: Robert Marlin

This counter display serves as a dispenser for rolls of tear-off cards of stickers, allowing a very small space to hold a large inventory.

Advertiser: USA Today
Producer: The Howard Marlboro Group, New York

This floor stand was part of a broad program designed to gain acceptance of a new newspaper among both readers and advertisers. The unit is easy to stock with current issues, and makes it easy for a consumer to select a paper to purchase.

Advertiser: Uchida of America
Producer: Glasheen Advertising, New York
Designer: Barbara Montgomery

This corrugated prepack floor display sets up quickly, and allows the customer to easily pick his favorite color of blister-packed ball point pen.

Advertiser: M. Grumbacher Inc.
Producer: Melrose Displays Inc.,
Passaic, NJ

This unit, only 30" square, holds 64 different styles and sizes of artists' paper. Made of individual pre-welded modules, it can stack to any configuration, and the casters make it easy to move around in the store. Wooden graphic panels slide in and out of channels for quick change-over.

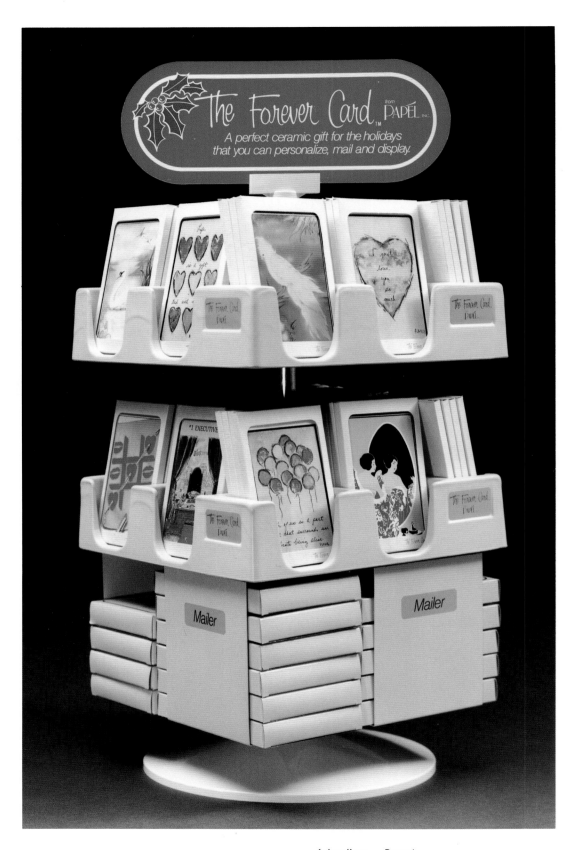

Advertiser: Papel
Producer: Trenmark, La Mirada, CA
Designer: Yuri Kucyna

This unit, designed for ceramic greeting cards, can expand from a counter display into a six-tier floor stand. The light color of the material helps the colorful greeting cards stand out.

Advertiser: Carlton Cards
Producer: The Acorn Group, Chicago

For a more permanent appearance, this display has its edges covered with plastic extruded chrome strips. The corrugated shelving is rigid enough to hold the product, and the header is removable.

Advertiser: Uchida of America
Producer: Glasheen Advertising, New York
Designer: Barbara Montgomery

This simple plastic holder holds six dozen pencils in a minimum space with maximum impact.

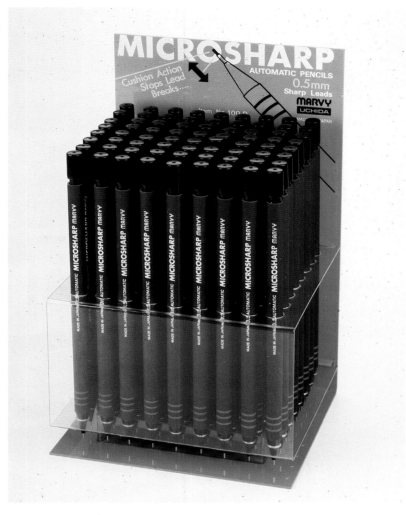

Advertiser: Bic Pen Corporation
Producer: Henschel-Steinau, Inc., Englewood, NJ

Striking use of a smoked injection-molded plastic pedestal and trays compartmentalize 360 pieces of the different writing instrument products into an eye-catching merchandising display that takes up only one square foot of counter space. The products are stepped or angled to provide visibility and accessibility. The unit is shipped completely assembled.

Advertiser: Pilot Pen
Producer: Thomson-Leeds Co. Inc., New York

This counter unit holds 12 boxes, each with 12 pens. Easy loading from stock, since all the retailer must do is remove the top of each box of pens, and slip the bottom with the pens, in place. The colorful pen tops show up brilliantly against the black background of the display.

Advertiser: Shachihata Inc.
Producer: Brinker Displays,
East Orange, NJ

This five-sided display holds a wide range of rubber stamps, and speeds up the selection process by the customer or the salesman. It rotates on a wooden cabinet which holds extra stock.

Advertiser: Sanford Corp.
Producer: Visual Marketing Inc., Chicago
Designer: Larry Zock

To merchandise stock rubber stamps for the office as an impulse item, this prepacked countertop display comes in bright red to attract attention in an office supply store, the stamps are positioned angled upwards to make their names easily read, and they are arranged alphabetically, so the customer can easily see what is available and select what he needs. There is space behind the graphic header for additional stock. All of the 60 items in the line have been displayed in only 87 square inches.

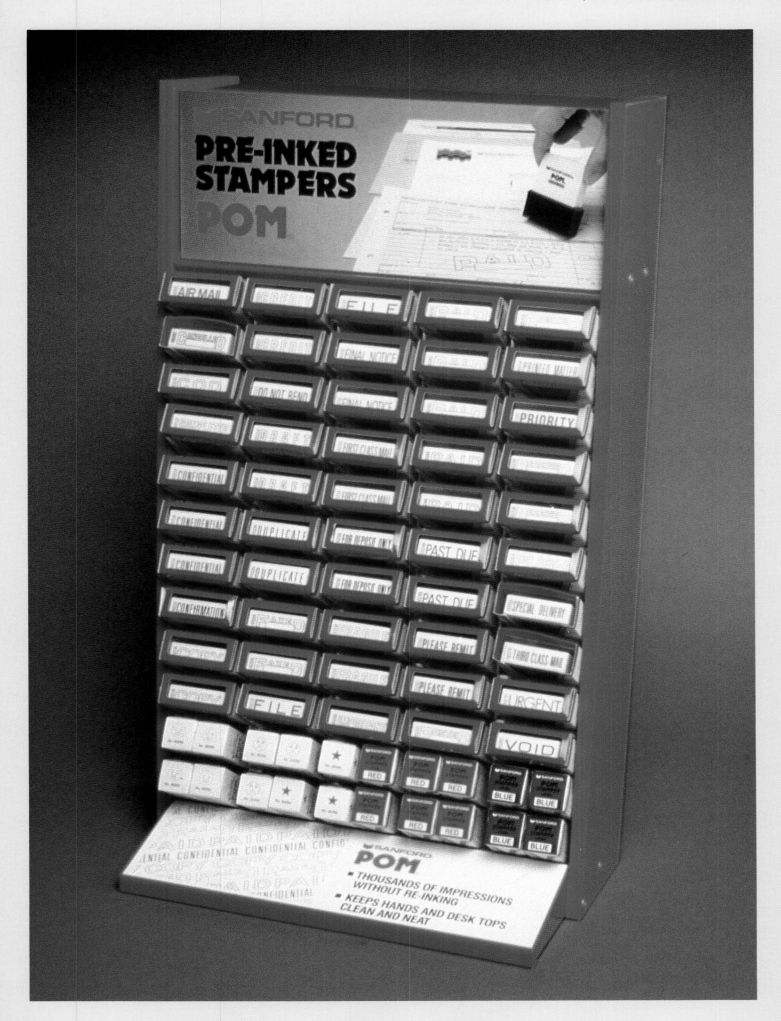

Advertiser: Gillette Co.
Producer: Trans World Marketing,
East Rutherford, NJ

This elegant display matches the upscale image of the Waterman pen. The vacuum formed outer casing features fine detailing and gold hot stamp decorations, while the gold-flocked inner trays of styrene, each holding 13 pens with elastic cord, present the product in a suitable setting. There is room between the two trays for a product brochure and a flip chart kit.

Advertiser: Uchida of America
Producer: Glasheen Advertising, New York
Designer: Barbara Montgomery

This counter stand utilizes the bright colors of the product to be the attention getter.

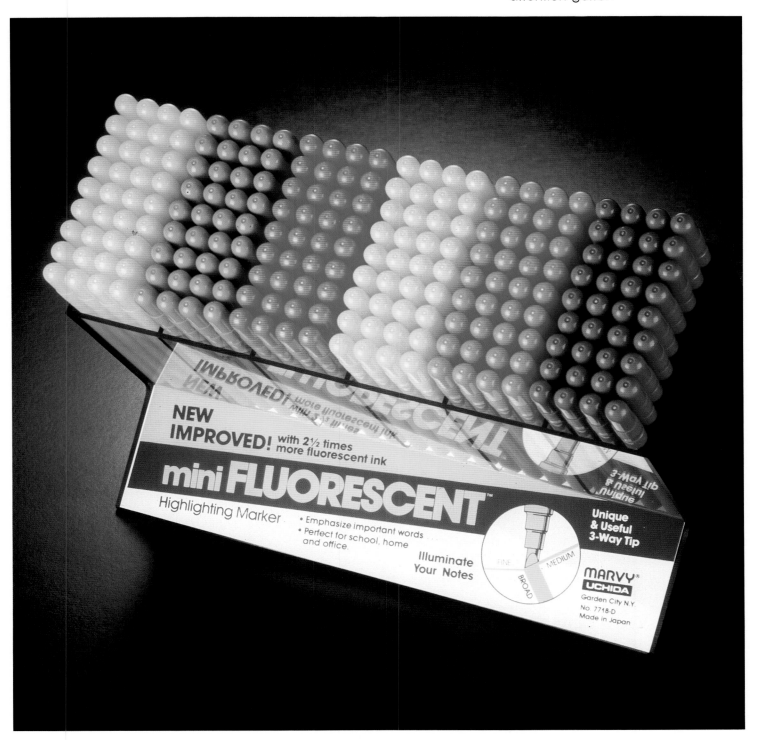

Advertiser: Sheaffer Eaton
Producer: Brinker Displays,
East Orange, NJ

This elegant countertop display is very versatile, allowing the retailer to change the product included, as well as the header.

Advertiser: Computerland
Producer: Trenmark, La Mirada, CA

Designed to display after market accessories for computers, this island display has slat-wall backgrounds that can be fitted with shelves, hooks, and even enclosed glass showcases.

Advertiser: Micro Pro
Producer: Patrick H. Joyce and Associates, Des Plaines, IL

This permanent counter display holds computer software in a manner which makes it easy for the customer to make his selection. A built-in looseleaf notebook can be used for product sheets or manual extracts.

Advertiser: Uchida of America
Producer: Glasheen Advertising, New York
Designer: Barbara Montgomery

This box of two dozen blister-packed rolls of tape is a counter or shelf display unit with the minimum of installation and set up time.

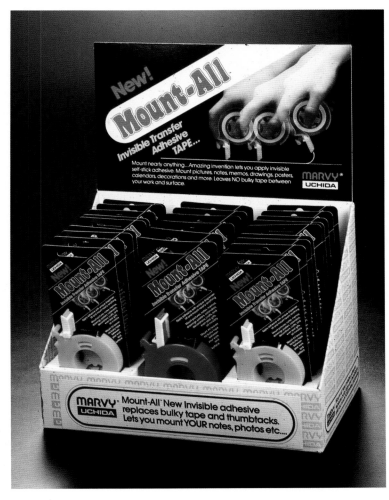

Advertiser: Uchida of America
Producer: Glasheen Advertising, New York
Designer: Barbara Montgomery

With the addition of a header, this product carton becomes an effective and easy to set set up counter display.

Advertiser: 3M Household & Hardware
                   Products Division
Producer: The Acorn Group, Chicago

The lithographed headers remind the consumer that they may need wrapping tapes, and offer a premium for picking Scotch Brand. The large capacity, on the hooks and in the dump, minimize the restocking requirements during a busy retail season.

Advertiser: Smith Corona
Producer: Ledan Inc., New York

This two-sided counter unit can come apart to form two units that can hang on a wall or on pegboard. A shallow injection-molded plaque heads the top of the display, while the unit itself is of vacuum-packed styrene and pegboard with metal hooks.

Advertiser: Shachihata Inc.
Producer: Brinker Displays,
East Orange, NJ

The counter display for custom-made, self-inking rubber stamps permitted the customer to see the quality of the stamp, to judge its output, and to see the ink colors available.

P-O-P TRENDS IN THE FINANCIAL SERVICES INDUSTRY

GERALD L. BAKER
Bank of America
SAN FRANCISCO, CA

To understand better what changes will occur in financial services merchandising over the next ten years, it's first necessary to consider several phenomena currently occurring in the industry, and appreciate the reasons why they are occurring.

Deregulation of financial services began gathering momentum in the early '80s and now, like most other businesses, financial institutions face strong domestic and foreign competition. Many institutions were unprepared for the new competitive environment and were slow to respond.

Many are still saddled with expense structures that are too high, revenues that are flat or declining, and profit margins that are too thin to support old established habits. All of this means that financial institutions must change the way they do business if they are to survive profitably. And nowhere will the changes be more obvious than in the marketing, merchandising, and selling of financial services.

The most significant industry change is the rapidly developing "sales revolution," a phenomenon taking many forms, but usually beginning with an attempt to inculcate the staff with a sales culture—a more aggressive attitude toward getting and retaining business. Often this is followed with an increased focus on cross-selling existing as well as new products and services, and on taking greater advantage of the selling opportunities that exist when customers are physically inside the institution. It all comes down to getting more sales revenue per square foot of office space, much as consumer products retailers have done for years. Consequently, there will be increasing use of merchandising and point-of-sales materials in branch locations, so that by the next decade, sales and merchandising skills will be well-honed in the successful financial institutions of the '90s.

P-O-P merchandising will be designed to fit into a variety of physical structures. Banking services will be offered to consumers in full-service, limited-service, and self-service locations ranging from free-standing kiosks and buildings to simple store-fronts; in larger facilities with high transaction volumes and in smaller sales offices promoting specialized services. They'll also be offered electronically, through a combination of automated teller machines (ATMs) and home and office computers, as well as by telephone and mail. But despite the variety of facilities, configurations, and financial services delivery alternatives, there will be several P-O-P areas that will receive major focus: exterior merchandising, interior selling environments, product and service selling areas, and promotional merchandising.

Product and Service Selling Areas

Most financial institutions have realized they can no longer be all things to all people, serving all markets with a full line of products and services. The size of the facility will depend on the market, so expect more specific product and service freestanding modules to allow expansion or contraction of services, especially for self-service products.

Internal space will be divided into selling areas, self-served and self-service, traditional and non-traditional, and third-party services. The key selling areas will be the vestibule or entrance foyer, the information or new accounts area, the loan and officer platform, and the tellerline or transactional area.

Each "selling" area provides the financial institution an opportunity to capture the customer's attention, create interest in a specific product or service, and establish an environment for the branch sales staff to advance the selling process. These areas will be considered prime or premium selling space. Therefore, increasing investment will be made in merchandising fixtures and displays to take maximum advantage of them and the opportunities they present to sell and cross-sell customers.

And as deregulation of financial services allows new, non-traditional services to be offered, and financial institutions pursue alternatives to earn income from compatible third-party businesses, new merchandising concepts will evolve. This could result in a lot of experimentation at many institutions. There will likely be graphic and style conflicts between emerging corporate and brand images and individual production promotions. But eventually, the successful institution will succeed in establishing a graphic design and style that helps create the overall branch selling environment, while matching the specific merchandising components used to sell featured and promoted products and services.

Promotional Merchandising

In order to make better use of sales staff time, there will be greater focus on selling and merchandising "core" products, the products and services most wanted or needed by customers. Since selling space will be considered extremely valuable, only high-ticket products, or those in high demand, will be visibly merchandised and actively promoted.

The calendar year will be divided into specific selling periods—months or quarters—that take advantage of seasonal product opportunities or local market needs. Only one product or several related products will be advertised, promoted, and merchandised during each period. All promotional material will be coordinated under one common theme and graphic style. As a result, there will be much less promotional clutter in the branch or conflicting selling messages in the media.

In-branch merchandising materials will be elaborate, requiring complete merchandising kits and instructional details. Whereas in the '80s window banners, posters, and brochures were typical in-branch promotional materials, in the '90s freestanding prefabricated promotional displays of every size, type, and description will become commonplace. More than one version of the display and related materials will be created in order to more correctly appeal to the market segment served by the branch.

The majority of financial products are not purchased impulsively; they are well-considered decisions. Since the decision-making period for the customer can be quite long, and the competitive alternatives so numerous, the successful financial institution must use every communications tool at its disposal to retain and build business. Remembering that the best prospect is the customer you currently have, it's no wonder that point-of-sale merchandising will receive increasing focus by the financial services marketers of the '90s.

Advertiser: Magnum Corporation
Producer: Lintas Kuala Lumpur, Malaysia
Designer: Albert Choo

A variety of elements were developed to help introduce a new computerized, four-digit lottery, and to explain how it works to potential purchasers.

COMPUTERISED

4d 電腦萬字

ONE STOP SERVICE
到一家代理處就行了

BETTING LIMITS
可買盡一個字

ADVANCE SALES
可預購萬字

 **SELLING HOURS**
營業時間更長

FAIR DRAWS
當眾搖珠開彩

GUARANTEED FULL PAYMENT
每期獎金保証派足

MAGNUM-ENE
MAKING OPPORTUNITIES WORK, FOR YOU.
萬能為您造萬福

Advertiser: Magnum Corporation
Producer: Lintas Kuala Lumpur, Malaysia
Designer: Albert Choo

A variety of elements were developed to help introduce a new computerized, four-digit lottery, and to explain how it works to potential purchasers.

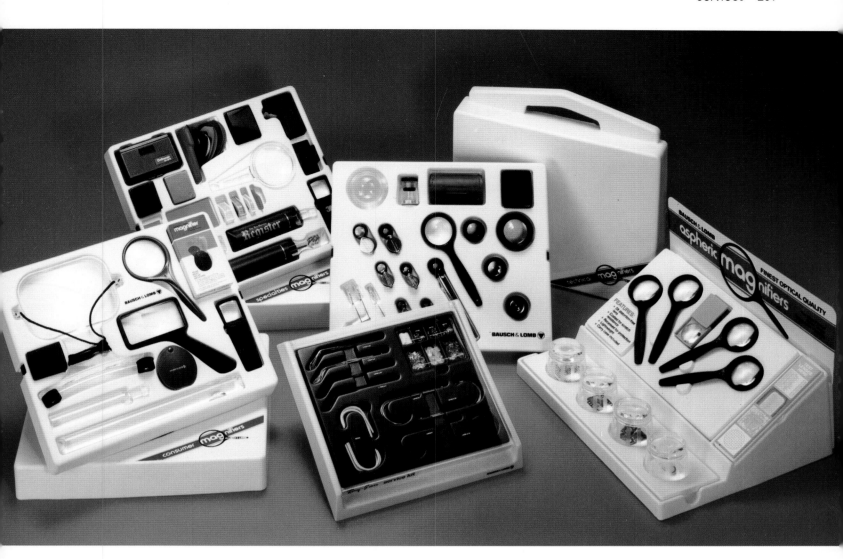

Advertiser: Bausch & Lomb
Producer: David Brace Displays Inc.,
Lancaster, NY

These units, using a versatile
molded plastic vacuum-formed
process, can produce a wide
variety of structures, including
counter displays, salesmen's kits,
and opticians' repair kits.

Advertiser: Citicorp Banks
Producer: AMD Industries Inc., Chicago

To call attention to the availability of literature to be taken by the consumer, this three-sided pylon can be placed wherever there is traffic. The rotating header attracts attention.

Advertiser: Citibank SA
Producer: Creative Displays Inc., Chicago

This new concept in banking—the
Time Saver—is a free-standing
booth and drop box, designed for
a high traffic bank or a lobby.

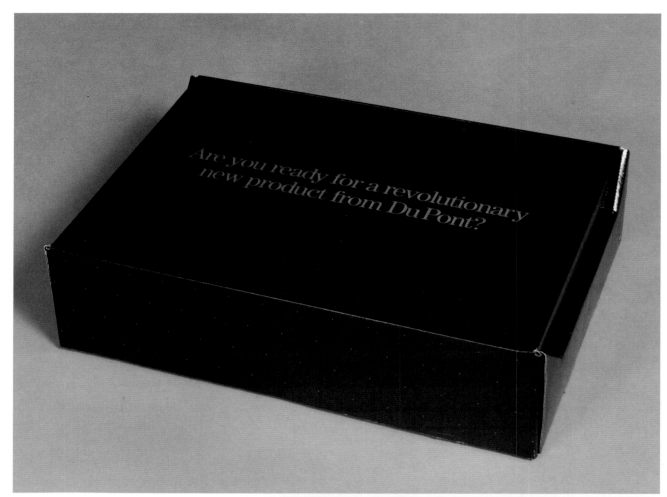

Advertiser: DuPont
Producer: Associated Packaging Inc.,
West Deptford, NJ
Designer: William Manteufel

To introduce a new pillow, not only a new item for DuPont, but also a breakthrough in pillow technology, the company used a sample in a corrugated box as part of its demonstration kit. The black exterior contrasted with the gold foil lining.

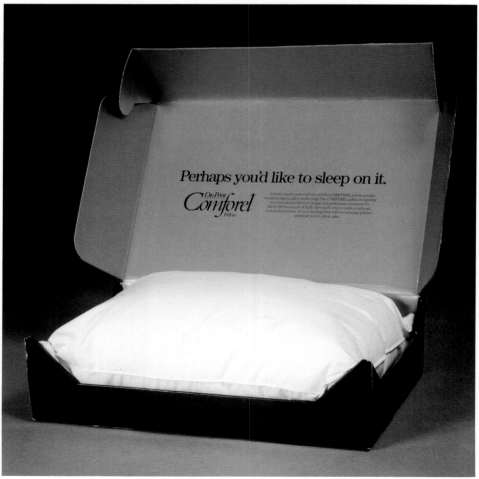

Advertiser: Woolworth Express

Producer: Advanced Interactive Video Inc., Columbus, OH

This triangular kiosk, matching the decor of the new type of store for which it was designed, has a 35" color monitor facing entering customers, as well as a large back-lit poster. The large screen shows made-for-television commercials of brands that are available. The interactive 19" monitor, facing into the store, is where the action is. A series of images explains what is on the system and how to use it. The consumer touches one of the categories—helpful information, coupons, sales, or survey—and gets further instructions. Coupons and other materials can be printed to order and issued to the consumer immediately.

Advertiser: Beefeater Gin; Safeguard
Producer: Manifestations Specialty
Promotions Inc., Carlsbad, CA

These two counter cards illustrate
how this unique metallic paper
product whose pattern changes as
you walk by can be used.

Advertiser: American Express Co.
Producer: Trans World Marketing,
East Rutherford, NJ

This floor stand was designed to get promotional literature in key target markets, like car rental agencies, department stores, and shopping malls. The brushed metal finish and simulated graphite panels produced an upscale image and made the unit compatible with contemporary store interiors. The graphic panel is interchangeable, and the space is offered in return for placement. At Alamo Rent-A-Car, for example, a magnetic bulletin board allowed the company to promote daily specials. A merchandise certificate, good at that mall, was offered credit card applicants, helping build return traffic for the mall.

Advertiser: Hertz Corporation
Producer: Marketing Displays Inc., Farmington Hills, MI

These signs are designed for curbside identification of urban offices, using a portable sign that can be moved indoors after business hours. The weighted base keeps it stable in high winds, and the frame folds for easy handling and compact storage.

Advertiser: Old Kent Bank & Trust Co.
Producer: Creative Displays Inc., Chicago

This simple literature holder, designed for a wide variety of outlets, comes in one piece, ships flat, and folds together for use.

Advertiser: Chicopee
Producer: Associated Packaging Inc.,
West Deptford, NJ
Designer: Peter Hindre

This sales kit, made of corrugated to look like a tool kit, provided a product demonstration, carried samples of product in various sizes, as well as sales literature and give aways. It was different enough so that it aroused customer interest.

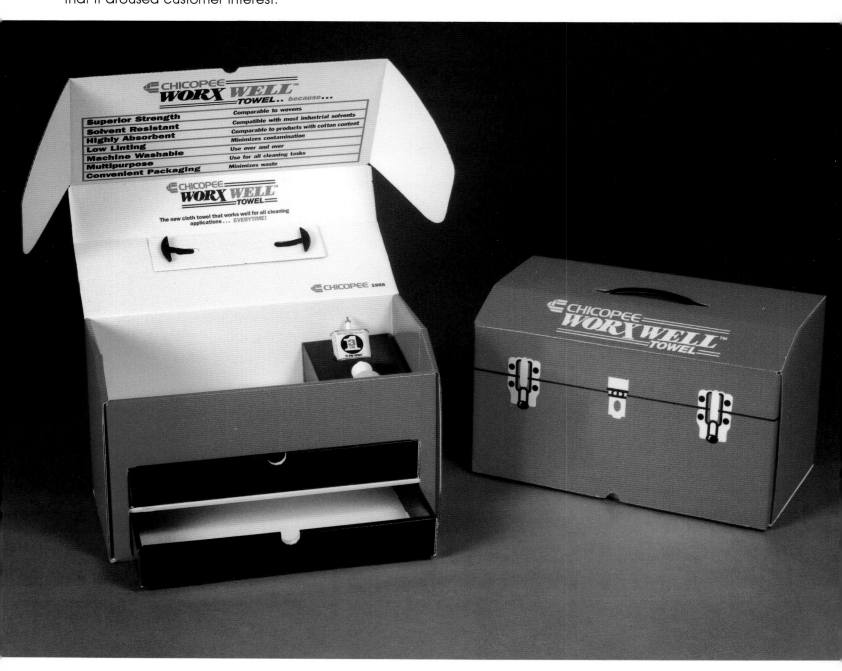

Advertiser:	Safeway Stores
Producer:	Corky Chapman Associates, San Francisco
Designer:	Joe Ugie

An inexpensive mobile, printed directly on board, die cut, folded and stapled, with a score at the top to prevent warping.

SAFEWAY Explore the Store mobile

KIT contains, 1 header, 1 rope, 1 hook & cord, two 2" barbettes, two 4" barbettes.

NOTE: Fold down along the top of the header to prevent warping.

Tie string securely to the "eye" of the hook.

...two copy "balloons" printed on both sides, and one "explorer"

Staple both sides of the explorer and the header to each other where indicated. Use your judgement.

© 1984

Advertiser:	Safeway Stores
Producer:	Corky Chapman Associates, San Francisco
Designer:	Patrick O'Daniels

For a special in-store promotion that would last only one to two weeks, an inexpensive mobile, using existing art, was developed that avoided the cost of duplex mounting on board. The enlarged art was printed on a large sheet of .024 pt SBS board, die cut and folded in half. Instead of being glued at the plant, the unit was stapled in the store and held together with barbettes. The header is 34" x 15".

INDEX

DESIGNERS

PRODUCERS

A

B

C

D

E